HISTORY OF GRAND CANYON NATIONAL PARK

By

Margaret M. Verkamp

A Thesis

submitted to the faculty of the

Department of History

in Partial fulfillment of

the requirements for the degree of

Master of Arts

in the Graduate College

University of Arizona

1940

A publication of the
Grand Canyon Pioneers Society
P.O. Box 2372
Flagstaff, Arizona 86003-2372
First Printing 1993
ISBN 0-933269-06-4 Softcover

Library of Congress Number 93-079941

Cover photo: Verkamp Store, Grand Canyon, Arizona, circa 1910, Grand Canyon National Park collection. Margaret M. Verkamp photo, courtesy Mike Verkamp.

PREFACE TO REPRINT

When I began reading various histories of the Grand Canyon, I often came upon references to the *History of Grand Canyon National Park*, by Margaret M. "Peggy" Verkamp. A search at the Flagstaff Library led me to discover that the reference was an unpublished master's thesis, but it was unavailable in their collection. As time went by I continued to encounter references to this paper. Fortunately for me, I had made the acquaintance of Steve Verkamp through membership in the Grand Canyon Pioneers Society. Steve graciously loaned me a copy of the manuscript, and allowed me to make a xerographic copy for my own collection. Unfortunately Steve's copy was about a fifth carbon copy (do you remember carbon paper?) on onion skin paper. The carbon was a little light and didn't copy too well, making it hard to read, and impossible to re-copy.

In order to make a more readable copy, and perhaps make it available for others, I decided to transcribe the thesis on a word processor. If you have ever seen me type, you would understand what a monumental task this was. Then I attempted the even bigger task of creating an index for the thesis, (I now have a great deal of respect for people who create indices). The task remained incomplete for several years until recently when the subject of Peggy's thesis came up during a meeting of the Grand Canyon Pioneers Society. Several members said that they never had the opportunity to read her paper. After I told them that I had the complete thesis transcribed in electronic format, I had to accept the challenge to complete the index and format the paper for publication by the Grand Canyon Pioneers Society. The *History of Grand Canyon National Park*, by Margaret M. Verkamp, is the first volume of what we hope will become a continuing "Collectors Series".

My special thanks to Paul Sweitzer who prepared the following biographical sketch, to Mike Verkamp who provided the cover photograph and portrait of Peggy, and to Steve Verkamp, John G. "Jack" Verkamp, Jeanne Schick, Bill and Sibyl Suran, and Carol Furey-Werhan who encouraged me to complete this task. I hope many readers will find pleasure in having this interesting history paper available for their research and collection.

The Grand Canyon Pioneers Society was organized to preserve the history of the Grand Canyon region. Society membership consists of individuals who share this common interest. The society conducts historical tours for members and guests, and publishes a bi-monthly newsletter. The society is actively engaged in collecting and archiving documents, photographs and other memorabilia. The collection is housed in the Specials Collections and Archives at the Cline Library, Northern Arizona University. You are invited to join us.

Ronald W. Werhan
Parks, Arizona
June, 1993

Margaret M. "Peggy" Verkamp
February 14, 1913
September 1, 1989

PEGGY VERKAMP: GRAND CANYON HISTORIAN

By Paul Sweitzer

I am delighted the Grand Canyon Pioneers Society has decided to publish "History of Grand Canyon National Park," a thesis written in pursuit of a master's degree from University of Arizona.

The author, longtime Grand Canyon resident and businesswoman, Margaret Mary "Peggy" Verkamp, was awarded the degree in history in 1941. Bound copies of the unpublished thesis have reposed in the library at UofA and in other major libraries for years as a primary source on the history and creation of Arizona's oldest National Park.

No one was better qualified to write this history than Peggy Verkamp, who died September 1, 1989, at her home in Sedona, after a long, productive life; a life lived quietly, but with never-ending purpose.

The thesis is not an exciting romance novel. It is a masterful piece of scholarship. Nonetheless, it contains excitement and romance as it describes the arrival of the Spaniards on the Canyon's rim in 1540 and the time when the author's father established his famous "store on the rim" in a tent in 1898; the first commercial venture of its kind at the Grand Canyon.

Peggy, born in Flagstaff on February 14, 1913, spent most of her adult life in that store. She was a presence there, seated quietly in a little office just off the main floor busy with some desk work and keeping a caring eye on visitors, as customers in the store were always called.

John George Verkamp, her father, made the store his fulltime enterprise in 1936, after a lifetime of enterprise that included livestock raising. He died unexpectedly in 1944 and Peggy, his oldest child, her mother, Catherine, and her sisters took over the store until 1945 when a brother John G. "Jack" Verkamp, Jr., was released from World War II military service.

Peggy grew up in Flagstaff where she attended St. Anthony's Catholic School. She then attended Loretto Academy, in El Paso, Texas, for part of her high school education and graduated from Loretto Academy, in Santa Fe, New Mexico. She attended Loretto Heights College, Denver, Colorado, before returning to Flagstaff to attend Northern Arizona University.

She received a bachelor's degree in education from NAU in 1935 and subsequently taught school in McNary, Flagstaff and Grand Canyon. Her interest in education never waned. In the 1950's she and Arizona's legendary U.S. Senator Carl Hayden worked together to obtain federal funds to found and build Grand Canyon High

School. She served for nine years as a member of the board of trustees of the Grand Canyon Unified School District.

Her interest in and love of Grand Canyon prompted her to take up color photography. A portfolio of her stunning pictures of The Canyon was published with U.S. National Park Service naturalist Louis Schellbach writing the commentary.

From 1937-87, Peggy was at "the store on the rim." She counted her other interests as her nieces and nephews and caring for her mother, as Catherine advanced graciously into old age.

Peggy always spoke of The Canyon with love and reverence; a reverence that amounted to awe, even if she did see it virtually every day of her life for 50 years.
That feeling comes through in her thesis.

Paul Sweitzer . . .
. . . is a native of Flagstaff who first saw and remembers Grand Canyon more than 50 years ago. He has worked in many capacities at The Arizona Daily Sun, Flagstaff's community newspaper, for more than 30 years. He knew Peggy Verkamp and counted her a friend.

ABSTRACT

The explorations of the Spaniards, American trappers and United States survey parties along the Colorado River between 1540 and 1890 included the Grand Canyon in several instances. Their reports aroused little interest in the Canyon because no details or descriptions were given, beyond the mention of its existence. The arrival of the railroad in northern Arizona had a greater influence, because it brought settlers into the region. Among the newcomers were many prospectors to whom the Canyon offered a rich field for activity. The prospectors began working at the Canyon about 1885 and were soon followed by mining companies. Mining proved to be unprofitable and began to decline about 1900. Tourist travel, which developed simultaneously with the mining interest, grew rapidly after the turn of the century. The struggle of the mining concerns to prolong their life is the story of continual controversy between them and the railroad and the National Government. Due to the national aspect of the tourist trade, the Government finally took over full control by creating the Grand Canyon a national park. When the Government's control was firmly established, the mining interests were ousted in favor of the railroad, which was placed under strict regulation by the Government for the benefit of the tourists.

PREFACE

In this presentation of a chronological history of Grand Canyon National Park stress has been placed upon events following its permanent settlement. Previous to this time its history had little bearing upon its eventual creation as a national park.

The simultaneous growth of the mining industry and tourist travel at Grand Canyon caused little conflict until the former began to decline. In an effort to save their holdings, the miners attempted to encroach upon the tourist business operated by the railroad and its subsidiaries. Bitter controversies resulted.

This thesis follows the development of the mining and tourist business and their conflict, which resulted in the need for governmental control. This control was not achieved easily. Due to local opposition and national indifference its growth was slow, advancing by gradual steps, through the efforts of individual men.

TABLE OF CONTENTS

CHAPTER I   THE PERIOD OF EXPLORATION 1540-1880 1
Spanish Conquistadors 1
Spanish Missionaries 3
American Trappers 5
Official and Semi-Official Explorations of the Colorado River 7

CHAPTER II OPENING OF THE GRAND CANYON REGION 9
Early American Visitors to the Grand Canyon 9
Coming of the Railroad to Northern Arizona 10
First Attempts to Build a Railroad to the Grand Canyon 12
Prospecting at Grand Canyon 14

CHAPTER III MINING AT GRAND CANYON 16
Prospectors 16
Mining Companies 17

CHAPTER IV TOURIST TRAVEL AT GRAND CANYON 22
Early Stage Lines 22
Hotels at Grand Canyon 23
Curios and Photography 26
North Rim 27

CHAPTER V THE BRIGHT ANGEL TRAIL 29
Controversies Over Toll Collection 29
Coconino County Acquires Possession of the Trail 31
The Railroad's Attempts to Gain Control of the Trail 31
The National Government's Purchase of the Trail 33
Controversies Over Ralph Cameron's Mining Claims 35

CHAPTER VI GRAND CANYON NATIONAL PARK 37
Creation of Grand Canyon Forest Reserve 37
Creation of Grand Canyon National Monument 39
Creation of Grand Canyon National Park 41
National Park Service Control of the Grand Canyon National Park 43
Later Developments Under Federal Direction of the Grand Canyon National Park ...44

BIBLIOGRAPHY 46

INDEX 53

CHAPTER I THE PERIOD OF EXPLORATION 1540-1880

Spanish Conquistadors

The Grand Canyon of Arizona was first seen by white men in 1540. An expedition of Spaniards under Francisco Vasquez de Coronado had been sent from Mexico by Viceroy Antonio de Mendoza to explore the country north of Culiacan in an effort to find the seven rich cities of Cibola. The Spaniards had heard rumors of these cities since 1530. In that year Nuño de Guzman had attempted to reach them by an overland route north through Mexico, but found the mountains of the province of Culiacan too difficult to pass through.

Again in 1536 four survivors of Panfilo de Narvaez's Florida expedition of 1528 arrived in Vera Cruz bearing more accounts of the seven cities of Cibola. They had received their information from the Indians of the Sonora Valley. Panfilo de Narvaez had received a patent authorizing him "to explore, conquer and colonize the country between Florida and the Rio de Palmas" an extent of territory comprising all the land bordering on the Gulf of Mexico[1]. Practically his entire expedition was either lost at sea, or killed by the Indians. Only four men, Cabeza de Vaca, Alonso del Castillo Maldonado, Andres Dorantes and Estevan, a negro, escaped. After seven years of wandering through the country along the Texas gulf coast these four men managed to find their way to the coast of the Gulf of California in northern Mexico. Continuing southeast, parallel with the coast, they met some slave hunters in the Sinaloa Valley[2] who directed them to Vera Cruz. At Vera Cruz they repeated what they had heard concerning the cities of Cibola. Their story reached Viceroy Mendoza who summoned Dorantes for an interview. After questioning him, Mendoza determined to send an expedition to find the cities. In 1539 he sent a Franciscan Friar, Marcos de Niza, with Estevan as a guide, to explore a route.

Estevan traveled two weeks in advance of Fray Marcos, and upon reaching the village of Cibola was killed by the natives. News of his death frightened the Friar's Indians, who refused to advance. It is reported that they took Marcos to a small hill from which he could see Cibola at a distance. He said that "it has a very fine appearance for a village, the best that I have seen in these parts....Judging by what I could see from the height where I placed myself to observed it, the settlement is larger than the city of Mexico."[3]

Marcos' report encouraged Mendoza to send the Coronado Expedition the following year. This latter was undertaken on a large scale. There were the land party of about three hundred Spaniards and several hundred Indians under Francisco Vasquez de Coronado[4] and a fleet of three ships under Hernando de Alarcon. The latter was to sail up the Gulf of California.

After five months of toilsome travel Coronado's army arrived at Cibola. It proved to be a poor mud village inhabited by the Zuni Indians. The army conquered the town and remained there for two or three weeks resting and subduing the natives.

---

[1]Winship, G.P., "The Coronado Expedition", *14th Annual Report of the Bureau of Ethnology, p.346.*

[2]Bishop, M.G., *The Odyssey of Cabeza de Vaca*, pp. 63-144.

[3]Winship, *op. cit.*, pp. 361-362.

[4]Ibid., pp. 378-379.

While they were stationed at Cibola, Coronado was told of some Indian towns to the west. He commissioned Don Pedro Tovar to take a small force and visit this province, which was called Tusayan. Tovar marched northwest for five days though uninhabited country until he reached Tusayan. From the natives he heard tales of a mighty river several days to the west.[5] Tovar returned to Cibola without hunting for the river. His report interested Coronado, who sent Don Garcia Lopez de Cardenas to find it. Casteñada describes the small expedition as follows:

> He (Cardenas) was well received when he reached Tusayan and was entertained by the natives, who gave him guides for his journey. They started from here loaded with provisions, for they had to go through a desert country before reaching the inhabited region, which the Indians said was more than twenty days journey. After they had gone twenty days they came to the banks of the river, which seemed to be more than three or four leagues above the stream which flowed between them. This country was elevated and full of low twisted pines, very cold and lying open toward the north, so that, this being the warm season, no one could live there on account of the cold. They spent three days on this bank looking for a passage to the river which looked from above as if the water was six feet across, although the Indians said it was half a league wide. It was impossible to descend, for after these three days Captain Melgosa and one Juan Galeras and another companion, who were the three lightest and most agile men, made an attempt to go down at the least difficult place, and went down until those who were above were unable to keep sight of them. They returned about four o'clock in the afternoon, not having succeeded in reaching the bottom on account of the great difficulties which they found, because what seemed to be easy from above was not so, but instead very hard and difficult. They said that they had been down about a third of the way and that the river seemed very large from the place which they reached, and that from what they saw, they thought the Indians had given the width correctly. Those who had stayed above had estimated that some huge rocks on the sides of the cliffs seemed to be about as tall as a man, but those who went down swore that when they reached these rocks they were bigger than the great tower of Seville. They did not go farther up the river because they could not get water. Before this they had had to go a league or two inland every day late in the evening in order to find water, and the guides said that if they should go four days farther it would not be possible to go on, because there was no water within three or four days.[6]

It is difficult from this account to determine the exact locality from which Cardenas saw the Grand Canyon of the Colorado. None of the authors on the subject

---

[5]Winship, *op. cit.*, p. 390.
[6]Winship, *op. cit.*, pp. 489-490

seem able to agree. It is quite evident that he must have reached the eastern end of the south rim of the Canyon from his description of the trees and altitude.

While Coronado was advancing overland, Alarcon with his small fleet sailed up the Gulf of California. At the head of the gulf he came to the mouth of the Colorado River. He is given the credit of having discovered this river, which he named the Buena Guia[7]. Leaving his ship in the gulf Alarcon ascended the river[8] in small boats[9]. Unable to contact Coronado, he descended the river and returned with his fleet to New Spain.

In the meantime, Coronado left Cibola and continued his explorations to the east. His operations extended as far east as eastern Kansas.[10] During this expedition of two years he found nothing of value. His men grew discontented and forced him to return to Mexico.

Spanish Missionaries

The next Spaniard to enter the country of the Grand Canyon was a Franciscan Friar, Augustin Rodriquez. In 1579 he received word from a captured Indian of a well populated country lying north, and his zeal for souls prompted him to visit these people.[11] His expedition left the mission at Santa Barbara and followed the Conchos River to the Rio Grande. They ascended the Rio Grande to the villages lying along its banks between Albuquerque and Santa Fe. In 1581 reports reached New Spain that Fray Rodriquez and the two priests who had accompanied him from Santa Barbara, had been killed by natives in the vicinity of Santa Fe. Don Antonio Espejo led an expedition to this region to ascertain the truth of this rumor.[12] After learning definitely that the priests had been killed, he turned to exploring the country. His reports of these explorations were responsible for the colonization of the Rio Grande country in 1598.

The settlements along the Rio Grande engaged the interest of the Spaniards for about one hundred years to the neglect of the Colorado River country. Oñate's expedition in 1604 was the last to visit the Colorado until 1701 when Father Kino, a Jesuit missionary in Pimeria Alta, explored the lower end of the river, establishing the fact that lower California was a peninsula and not an island.[13]

With the expulsion of the Jesuits from New Spain in 1767 the Franciscans took over the missions on the north Pacific Slope. Among the new missionaries was Father Francisco Garces, an enthusiastic explorer and missionary. He explored much of the territory covered by Father Kino and became thoroughly acquainted with it.

---

[7]James, G. W., *The Grand Canyon of Arizona*, p. 199.
[8]Simpson, J. H., *Coronado's March*, p. 10.
[9]It is not known how far upstream he went.
[10]Bolton, H. E. and Marshall, T. M., *The Colonization of North America*, pp. 46-47.
[11]Bolton, H. E., *Spanish exploration of the Southwest*, pp. 137-138.
[12]Bancroft, H. H., *History of Arizona and New Mexico*, p. 68
[13]Bolton, H. E., *Rim of Christendom*, pp. 484-486.

In 1774 when the Spaniards desired to find a land route to California they chose Father Garces as guide. He made two trips with Captain Juan Bautista de Anza to California. On the second, in 1776, he left the party and did some independent exploring up the Colorado River. Upon reaching the Mojave country he turned west and explored into California for two months. He next returned to the Colorado, crossed it and traveled east to the vicinity of Kingman. Turning north he arrived at Havasupai or Cataract Canyon, a branch of the Grand Canyon.

When Garces arrived at Havasupai Canyon the Indians insisted that he go down to visit the tribe living there. The following is a description of the descent given by the priest:

> I arrived at a rancheria, which is on the Rio Jabesua, which I named (Rio) de San Antonia, and in order to reach this place I traversed a strait which I call the Nuebo Canfran. This extends about three quarters (of a league), on one side is a very lofty cliff, and on the other a horrible abyss. This difficult road passed, there presented itself another and worse one, which obliged us to leave, I my mule and they their horses, in order that we might climb down a ladder of wood.[14]

Garces stayed in Cataract Canyon for a few days and then continued on his way to Tusayan. He traveled to the southeast and then to the east and, as he records,

> halted at the sight of the most profound caxones which ever onward continue; and within these flow the Rio Colorado. There is seen a very great sierra, which in the distance (looks) blue; and there runs from the southeast to the northwest a pass open to the very base, as if the sierra were cut artificially to give entrance to the Rio Colorado into these lands, I named this singular (pass) Puerto de Bucareli.[15]

From the Grand Canyon Father Garces continued in an easterly direction to Tusayan. Here he did not receive a very enthusiastic welcome and was warned to return.

The same year Father Garces visited the Grand Canyon, Father Escalante left Santa Fe in search of an overland route from that city to the mission at Monterey, California. He detoured northeast into Colorado and then turned northwest until he reached the valley of the Great Salt Lake. Winter overtook him before reaching the Sierra Nevada range, forcing him to return without reaching California.

On the return trip Escalante and his party returned southeastward until the Indians warned them of an impassable chasm ahead, the Grand Canyon. They were forced to change their route to the north and northeast to a ford of the Colorado of which the Indians had told them. It took them a week of hard labor to cross the river. This crossing is still called The Crossing of the Fathers.

---

[14]Coues, E., *On the Trail of a Spanish Pioneer*, Vol. ii, p. 337.

[15]Ibid., pp. 347-348. Bucareli was the name of the Viceroy of New Spain at that time.

The Spanish explorations of the Grand Canyon region came to an end with the expeditions of the Fathers Garces and Escalante. There were not a sufficient number of natives to warrant the establishment of missions and the country was not rich or fertile enough to entice settlers. Not until after the Louisiana Purchase and the Lewis and Clark Expedition did a white man again visit the region bordering the Grand Canyon. The acquisition of the vast territory in the northwest by the United States encouraged many American fur trappers to migrate west of the Missouri River.

American Trappers

In 1822 the Rocky Mountain Fur Company was formed by William Henry Ashley. In the spring of 1825 he went in search of beavers in the canyons of the Green River. This river rises in Wyoming and flows into southern Utah where it joins the Grand, forming the Colorado. Ashley's trip down the Green was very dangerous, because of the perpendicular walls rising from the water's edge, and the rapids in the river. He was the first man to attempt to navigate this river.[16] He was forced to abandon the trip when he lost his boat near the mouth of a small river which now bears his name.

In 1826 Ashley sold the Rocky Mountain Fur Company to three of his former employees; Jedediah S. Smith, David E. Jackson and William Sublette. Jedediah Smith did the exploring for the company and in 1826 found a new route to California. This route crossed the Sevier Valley from Utah Lake to the Virgin River, descending the Virgin to the mouth of the Mojave. Next the Colorado was crossed and the trail continued west across the desert to San Diego, California.

While the northern tributaries of the Colorado were being explored by the trappers, those of the south were not neglected. In 1826 Ewing Young led a party down the Gila to the Colorado. From the junction he went north along the Colorado over practically the same route followed by Father Garces in 1776. At Black Canyon the river gorge narrowed with perpendicular walls on either side forcing him and his party to climb the walls and continue along the rim of the canyons, one of which was the Grand Canyon. James Ohio Pattie, a member of the party, wrote a narrative of the trip and had the following to say of the journey from Black Canyon:

We reached a point of the river where the mountains shut in so close upon its shores, that we were compelled to climb a mountain, and travel along the acclivity, the river still in sight, and at an immense depth below us. Through this whole distance, which we judged to be, as the river meanders, one hundred leagues, we had snow from a foot to eighteen inches deep. The river bluffs on the opposite shore were never more than a mile from us. It is perhaps, this very long and formidable range of mountains, which has caused, that this country of Red river, has not been more explored, at least by the American people. A march more gloomy and heart wearing, to people hungry, poorly clad, and mourning the loss of their companions, cannot be imagined. Our horses had picked a little herbage and had subsisted on the bark of

---

[16]Chittenden, H. M., *The American Fur Trade of the Far West*, Vol. I, p.271.

shrubs. Our provisions were running low, and we expected every hour to see our horses entirely give out.

April 10, we arrived where the river emerges from these horrid mountains, which so cage it up, as to deprive all human beings of the ability to descend to its banks, and make use of its waters.[17]

Young's party continued up the Colorado River to the Grand. This they followed to the Continental Divide, which they crossed and descended on the eastern side to Santa Fe.

In 1829, Young sent a second trapping party into the Gila country. Christopher ("Kit") Carson was among the members and after the trapping had been done he and eighteen companions were sent to California. They followed a route northward for eight days, until they came upon the Grand Canyon. They remained only long enough to secure food from the Indians and then turned west crossing the Colorado near the mouth of the Mojave.[18]

The route followed by Carson and his party was one seldom used because of the lack of food and water along the way. The regular caravan route from Santa Fe to California was called the Old Spanish Trail. This route was first found in 1830 by William Wolfskill, one of Ewing Young's men. It started from Taos in a northeasterly direction to the head waters of the San Juan River, across the Grand and Green Rivers through the Gunnison Valley. From Gunnison Valley it crossed the western base of the Wasatch Range, then turned south through Mountain Meadows and across the Beaver Dam Mountains to the Virgin River. It followed the Virgin to the Colorado and then passed across the lower end of Nevada into California.[19]

[17]Flint, T. (ed.), *The Personal Narrative of James O. Pattie of Kentucky*, p. 97
[18]Vestal, S., *Kit Carson*, pp. 48-49.
[19]Bancroft, H. H., *History of Utah*, pp. 23-24

Official and Semi-Official Explorations of the Colorado River

Besides the organized companies engaged in the fur traffic along the tributaries of the Colorado, there were many independent trappers known as mountain men. They left few records, and as they worked alone their travels are difficult to trace. Some may have seen the Grand Canyon. Certainly most of them saw the Colorado River.

This river, whose erosive forces are responsible for so much of the unique beauty of the country through which it runs, was never very influential toward the opening of the country. This was due to the fact that it was not navigable along most of its course.

The United States Government became interested in it in 1850 as a possible means of transporting army supplies to southwestern army posts. The Bureau of Topographical Engineers of the War Department authorized a survey of the river under the direction of Lieutenant George H. Berby. In a row boat he ascended the river from the mouth to Fort Yuma, establishing the navigability of the river for that short distance.

The following year Captain Lorenzo Sitgreaves, of the United States Topographical Engineers, was sent to determine the source of the Zuni River and follow it to its junction with the Colorado. He was also instructed to follow the Colorado to the mouth.[20] Unable to follow along the banks of the Little Colorado, into which the Zuni empties, Sitgreaves turned southwest overland until he reached Bill Williams Fork. Thence he turned directly west and reached the Colorado River near the mouth of the Mojave. He hurried south, following the Colorado to Fort Yuma.[21]

In 1854 Lieutenant Amiel Weeks Whipple followed the Colorado upstream from the mouth of Bill Williams Fork to the Mojave and reported it navigable for small steam boats.

These various official and semiofficial explorations established the fact that the Colorado was navigable in parts. But the extent of navigation had not been determined. Therefore, in 1857 an expedition under Lieutenant Joseph Christmas Ives was sent by the War Department to explore the river with this end in view.

In his steamship the Explorer Ives ascended the Colorado to Black Canyon. At this point the rapids became so frequent and treacherous he was unable to take the ship farther. Leaving it, he and two other men rowed a skiff through Black Canyon to Vegas Wash. He proceeded no farther and reported the lower end of Black Canyon as the head of stream navigation.[22]

Following the expeditions upstream, two were made in 1869 and 1871-72 downstream by Major John Wesley Powell. The first was privately arranged by Powell with financial assistance from the Chicago Academy of Science. He had become interested in the geology of the canyons of the Colorado in 1867 while conducting a party of geologists into Colorado.

---

[20]Sitgreaves, Lorenzo, *Report of an expedition down the Zuni and Colorado Rivers*, p.4.
[21]Ibid., p.4ff.
[22]Ives, Joseph C., *Report upon the Colorado River of the West*.

Powell began his historic river trip on May 24, 1869, from Green River City, Wyoming, on the Green River. He arrived at the head of Grand Canyon two and a half months later. On August 31 he emerged from the Grand Canyon at the mouth of the Virgin River, where he ended his voyage.

Powell was not satisfied with the results of his first trip because many scientific instruments and records had been lost along the way. Therefore he determined to undertake a second expedition. With a new group of men and financial aid from the United States Government he set out from Green River Station in the fall of 1871. The trip was made in two stages. The first was from Green River Station to the Paria River. At the Paria the boats were cached and the party left the river to spend the winter at Kanab, Utah. In July, 1872, they continued to second half of the journey ending at Kanab Canyon, a side canyon of the Grand Canyon.[23]

The last official river expedition of the nineteenth century was that under Captain George M. Wheeler, in 1871. This expedition started upstream from Fort Mojave. After a month of laborious progress against rapids, the party finally reached the mouth of Diamond Creek. A land party was waiting for them with much needed food. Wheeler decided to end his explorations because of the great difficulties encountered.[24]

There is only one more expedition of any importance to be considered here. It is the one started by Frank Mason Brown in March, 1889, and completed the next year by Robert Brewster Stanton. These men, having conceived the idea of a railroad running through the canyons of the Colorado River, made their voyage to survey them for this purpose.

Brown's death a little below Lee's Ferry, ended the first attempt. The second under Stanton's direction completed the survey to the Gulf of California. He was the first man to cover the entire distance from the junction of the Grand and Green Rivers to the Gulf.[25] Stanton found that the construction of a railroad through the canyons of the Colorado was possible from an engineer's point of view, but quite impossible economically.

The period of exploration ended about 1880. During the span of three hundred and forty years after its discovery, the Grand Canyon was visited occasionally by white men in the course of their travels. These men were not particularly interested in the Canyon, and not until the arrival of the railroad in northern Arizona did people begin to take notice of it.

---

[23]Powell, J. W., *Report of Explorations in 1873 of the Colorado of the West and Its Tributaries*.

[24]Wheeler, G. M., *Report Upon United States Geographical Surveys West of the One Hundredth Meridian*, pp. 156-169.

[25]Freeman, L. R., *The Colorado River*, pp. 307-321.

CHAPTER II   OPENING OF THE GRAND CANYON REGION

Early American Visitors to the Grand Canyon

In 1919 the national government of the United States created the Grand Canyon of Arizona into a national park. Today hundreds of thousands of people from the four corners of the world visit this great natural wonder. To these tourists it is a playground, preserved solely for their enjoyment and that of the generations to follow them. Upon their first visit one question will enter their minds. How was it formed? For years scientists have been working to answer this question. There has been a considerable amount of literature written on this subject. But there are still two other questions which should be answered: Who were the men who opened up this great area and developed it? What chain of events has led up to its final creation as a national park?

The answer to these questions is the romantic story of the labor, hardships and fortitude of a small handful of men. To them must be given the credit of awakening the public interest in the existence of this scenic wonder. They were not all interested in it for its beauty alone, but whether they were or not, it was through their activity that it was made accessible to the tourist of today.

Until the closing decades of the nineteenth century the Grand Canyon was known to few people. Its remoteness was, of course, a great hindrance to its early development as a tourist attraction. Its lack of agricultural promise discouraged settlement. Therefore, this picturesque area lay, for over three centuries after its discovery by white men, undisturbed by human development.

It is true, a few daring men had wrestled with the river which winds its way through the Grand Canyon. An occasional trapping party would spend a few weeks along some of the side streams, but none of these men left anything permanent toward the future development of this area, unless it was a slowly growing interest in it, aroused by their accounts. Accounts of natural wonders, practically impossible of belief until actually witnessed.

The first permanent western inhabitant to see Grand Canyon from the south rim was Jacob Hamblin. In 1863 he followed the Moqui Trail along its rim from Cataract Canyon to the Hopi villages. Hamblin was a Mormon missionary who had been living at Mountain Meadows, Utah, since 1858. He is the same Mormon whom Lieutenant Joseph C. Ives mentions having seen near Mojave Valley, when he made his voyage up the Colorado River in 1857.[26]

For years Jacob Hamblin had been a roving Mormon missionary. His activities extended into California and Arizona, as well as large portions of Utah. In 1862 President Brigham Young sent him to the Hopi villages to conduct some of the Indians to a conference in Salt Lake City.[27] Hamblin traveled southwest from Utah, crossing the Colorado River at the mouth of Grand Wash. Having crossed the river, he traveled southeast to the foot of the San Francisco Mountains, and then east to the

---

[26]Ives, *op. cit.*, p.88.

[27]Jenson, A., *Church Chronology*, p.66.

9

Hopi villages. The return trip to Salt Lake was made by way of the Crossing of the Fathers. From the time Hamblin left Salt Lake until his return he had made a tour completely around the Grand Canyon.[28] This is the first record of such a trip.

Hamblin accompanied the Hopi Indians upon their return to their villages from Salt Lake the following year, 1863. They crossed the Colorado near the site of Pierce's Ferry.[29] Turning east they came upon Cataract Canyon, which they crossed, rather than take the long route around. From Cataract Canyon they followed the old Moqui Trail to the Hopi villages. This trail is the ancient route followed by the Moqui, Mojave, Havasupai and other Indian tribes in the east-west trade. In his record of the trip, Hamblin makes no mention of the Grand Canyon, but he must have seen it as the trail closely approaches the Canyon's rim in many places. This omission can probably be accounted for by the fact that he was on a business trip and any sight seeing he might have done was only incidental and not worthy of recording.[30]

As the Mormon missionary and settlement activities continued throughout southern Utah and northern Arizona, the Grand Canyon was probably visited several times by the Mormons, but not much notice was taken of it. It was not until the Atlantic and Pacific Railroad entered northern Arizona that the Grand Canyon was first opened up by men who established themselves permanently along its rim.

Coming of the Railroad to Northern Arizona

The Atlantic and Pacific Railroad reached Flagstaff, Arizona, in 1882. Although there had been a small settlement of stockmen there as early as 1876, it was the railroad which insured the permanency of this settlement. The railroad brought with it many eastern people, anxious to establish themselves in this newly opened country. Among them was Edward E. Ayer.

Ayer, a lumberman, initiated the first lumber company in Flagstaff, in 1882. This was the beginning of an industry which, together with the cattle and sheep business, developed Flagstaff into a thriving little town.

As the population of Flagstaff grew, its people became more and more interested in the scenic wonders within its vicinity. Stories of the Grand Canyon had been told by the few men who had seen and marveled at its grandeur. In February of 1884 Ayer employed Phillip and William Hull, who owned a sheep ranch several miles south of the Canyon, to act as his guides on a trip to see it. He is the first tourist on record to make the trip.[31] By summer of the same year a number of people were making the three day journey from Flagstaff to the Grand Canyon.

The enthusiasm of the Canyon visitors was so great that it soon became evident that it was destined to became a great tourist resort. One of the first men to foresee

---

[28]Jenson, *op. cit.*, p. 66.

[29]This ferry was first established by Harrison Pearce in 1876. The spelling has been since changed. Today Pierce's Ferry is a boat landing on Lake Mead, the original site of the ferry having been inundated by the lake.

[30]McClintock, J. H., *Mormon Settlement in Arizona*, pp. 69-70

[31]McClintock, J. H., *Arizona*, Vol. II, p. 557.

this was John Hance. He first saw the Canyon in 1883. At that time he was engaged in breaking horses for William Hull.[32] He was greatly impressed by the beauty of the Canyon and in 1884 homesteaded on the rim. He did so with the intention of building tourist accommodations.

Captain John Hance, as he was called, although no one is sure that he ever actually held such a rank in the army, was probably the Canyon's most colorful character. Little is known of his early life. He was a Native of Tennessee,[33] and during the Civil War joined the Confederate Army. Later he was taken prisoner by the Union forces and joined their army.[34] After the Civil War he came to Arizona from Missouri with an ox team. For several years he hauled fodder for the army horses at Camp Verde.[35] Just when he moved to northern Arizona is not definitely known.

At the Grand Canyon he became one of the best known tourist guides and entertainers. His entertainment consisted chiefly in telling tall stories to his guests. By 1885 Hance had taken possession of Glendale Springs on the rim of the Canyon, and with William Hull built a log cabin for tourists. His guests reached the Canyon by a road running out of Flagstaff. A description of the road appeared in the Arizona Champion of November 21st:

> The road from Grand Canyon to Flagstaff is in capital condition for traveling. Though little traveled it has a sound base and is not rough. It is not difficult to trace and there are no steep grades or declivities.[36]

Shortly after establishing his home on the rim Hance built a trail into the Canyon. The head of this trail was located a little west of his cabin, about sixteen miles east of the present Grand Canyon Village. It had been an old indian trail, and he worked it over so that it could be used by tourists to descend into the vast depths of the Canyon.

By 1886 Hance had his little tourist establishment well set up, but business evidently needed a little stimulus. He relied mainly on people of Flagstaff and its vicinity for his business. For several months he ran the following advertisement in the local paper:

> Being thoroughly conversant with all the trails leading to the Grand Canyon of the Colorado, I am prepared to conduct parties thereto at any time. I have a fine spring of water near my house on the rim of the Canyon, and can furnish accommodation for tourists and their animals.[37]

[32]Bass, W. W., *Adventures in the Canyons of the Colorado*, p. 5

[33]Nicholson, G. T., *The Grand Canyon of Arizona*, p. 109.

[34]Kolb, E., *Personal Interview*, March 18, 1940

[35]Lauzon, H., *Personal Interview*, March 22, 1940

[36]*Arizona Champion*, November 21, 1885.

[37]Austin, E., *Grand Canyon Items*, p. 1

Hance's business may have been rather slow at times, but this never worried him. He used the dull seasons to prospect. During the first few years of his residence at the Canyon he made a few small copper and asbestos discoveries. His chief gain from his prospecting tours was an intimate knowledge of the Canyon, which qualified him so well as a guide.

First Attempts to Build a Railroad to the Grand Canyon

While Hance was working in his limited way to build up the tourist travel to the Grand Canyon, some of Flagstaff's citizens were working on a scheme with the same end in view. They saw the possibility of attracting world wide tourist travel. Their idea was to run a railroad to the Canyon from Flagstaff. On December 31, 1886, the Flagstaff and Grand Canyon Railroad Company was organized.[38] The following June, while J. S. Morris, the president of the company, went East to make financial arrangements, a survey party began work east of Flagstaff.

The ambitious undertaking soon met with failure, not because of lack of enthusiasm on the part of its promoters, but because it was attempted too early. The Canyon was not well enough known and the men able to finance it could not be convinced of the future possibilities for such a railroad. The company dissolved, but the idea never died.

A second attempt was made in 1889. That year the Fifteenth Territorial Legislature passed an act "to encourage the construction of a railroad to the Grand Canyon of the Colorado." It provided:

> That any corporation duly organized and incorporated under the laws of this Territory which shall construct a railroad from some point upon the line of the Atlantic and Pacific Railroad... to some suitable point upon the Grand Canyon... shall be exempted, and every species of property, real, personal and mixed, owned, held, used or occupied by said company for the purpose of constructing, operating and maintaining said road shall be exempt from taxation of every kind and description whatsoever... during the process of construction and for the period of six years from and after the completion of said railroad; provided,... that this Act shall not apply to any corporation which does not in good faith commence the construction of said railroad within two years from the date of the passage of this act...[39]

In order to take advantage of this act a second railroad company was formed. Many of the Flagstaff men who had been members of the first one were interested in

---

[38]J. S. Morris was President: D. M. Riordan, Treasurer, S. A. Buckler, Secretary; P. P. Daggs, P. J. Brannen, T. A. Riordan, D. M. Riordan, J. W. Eddy, A. A. McDonnell and J. S. Morris, Directors. *Arizona Champion*, January 8, 1887.

[39]*Session Laws of the Fifteenth Legislative Assembly of the Territory of Arizona*, Act. 28, pp.37-38.

this one too. Through their efforts they succeeded in getting a number of eastern capitalists[40] to come to Flagstaff to look over the project personally. However, they did not secure the financial aid they were looking for and the company met with no greater success than its predecessor.

Two years later, 1891, Flagstaff made its final bid for a railroad to the Grand Canyon. That year a mass meeting of the townspeople was called to devise ways and means of constructing this line. The following resolutions were unanimously adopted:

    1.   We will extend support and co-operation to any individual or corporation who will construct such a line.

    2.   We pledge our services and influence in procuring the right-of-way through private property.

    3.   We will generously furnish what financial aid we can.[41]

This testimonial of the willingness of the people of Flagstaff to be of all possible help in the construction of a railroad to the Grand Canyon did not prove to be sufficient guarantee to entice any company to come in from the outside to undertake the project. One local company was formed, but never proceeded much beyond the act of drawing up articles of incorporation.[42] The fate of these various efforts to build such a railroad was always the same. The men with the foresight did not have the capital and those with the capital were unwilling to take the risk. It was not until the beginning of the twentieth century that a railroad was finally run in to the Grand Canyon, and even then it did not join the main line at Flagstaff.

---

[40]Charles L. Rickerson, John C. De La Verne and Ellis Wainwright, *Arizona Champion*, July 20, 1889.

[41]*Coconino Sun*, October 22, 1891.

[42]E. S. Gosney, David Babbitt, John V. Rhoades, C. M. Thurston, G. A. Bray, P. J. Brannen, and Edward M. Doe formed this company. *Record of Articles of Incorporation, Coconino County, Territory of Arizona*, Vol. I, pp. 12-13, County Recorder's Office, Flagstaff, Arizona.

Prospecting at Grand Canyon

The opening of the Grand Canyon to public travel brought to it not only tourists, but men interested in wresting their fortunes from its walls. Prospectors thought limitless wealth had been placed before them. They found traces of half a dozen or more different minerals in the cliffs and floor of the Canyon.

The earliest report of prospecting in the Grand Canyon is in 1874. That year William Ridenour and S. Crozier with two companions did a little prospecting, probably in the western end of the Canyon. They were not very successful, because of an attack by hostile Indians, who drove them away.[43]

Prospecting, however, began in earnest about 1885. From 1885 to 1891 individual prospectors wandered about the Canyon, both on the rim and down in the gorge. These were men of little or no capital who would spend their winters prospecting. They usually worked alone or in small groups. Some of these men; William Henry Ashurst, father of Senator Henry F. Ashurst, Ralph Henry Cameron, later United States Senator from Arizona, John Hance, Grand Canyon guide, and a few others, figured in the later development of the Canyon.

Prospectors are among the greatest day-dreamers. They are eternally on the verge of untold riches. Their faith and hope seem inexhaustible. The Grand Canyon prospectors were no exception. They thought they had found so much gold that if they were not careful they would be apt to flood the gold market and cause a drop in the price. Their enthusiasm converted many of the business men of Flagstaff. These men would "grubstake" the prospectors, who in turn would stake out claims for them.[44] The result is that many mines will be found recorded in the names of men who never did any of the prospecting.

The early prospectors expended a great deal of time and energy on their work. As it is impossible to take a pack animal into the Canyon except by trail, they had to build trails in order to work their claims. Most of the trails they built were old abandoned Indian trails. These they worked over to make passable for their animals.

The most eastern, or Tanner Trail was built by Seth B. Tanner, a Mormon pioneer,[45] about 1884 or 1885. The Hance or Red Canyon Trail was built by John Hance about 1884. He originally intended it to be used by tourists in descending into the Canyon, but later, upon his discovery of copper and asbestos directly across the Colorado River from the foot of his trail,[46] he lengthened it. These were the two earliest trails opened into the Canyon.

From 1885 to 1889 the prospectors and the tourists made their entry chiefly from Flagstaff. Her citizens were early convinced of the Canyon's possibilities of mineral development and tourist attraction. They made every effort to make her the gateway to this wealthy region. But Flagstaff had a competitor—Williams. Like Flagstaff,

---

[43]McClintock, *Arizona*, Vol. II, p. 401.

[44]Babbitt, C. J., *Personal Interview*, March 1, 1940.

[45]James, G. W., *In and Around the Grand Canyon*, pp. 242-245.

[46]Gilliland, R. P., *Personal Interview*, March 21, 1940.

Williams was first settled by stockmen about 1876. With the advent of the railroad it became a permanent center for lumbering and stock raising.[47]

In the early eighties there was little apparent interest in the Canyon among the people of Williams. A few of the railroad men had seen it at the mouth of Diamond Creek Canyon, which was reached by the road from Peach Springs. But their reports were rather vague and only a few of the more curious took the trouble to make the trip. William Wallace Bass was one of these men. In July of 1883 he arrived in Williams as an employee of the Atlantic and Pacific Railroad. In September of the same year he made his first visit to the Grand Canyon, approaching it from Williams.[48] He became very interested in it both for its beauty and its mineral wealth. However, it was not until about 1889[49] that he actually located there.

Mention is made here of Bass because later he became one of the leading men in the development of the Grand Canyon region, as a prospector and a tourist guide. However, between 1883 and 1889 neither he nor any of his fellow citizens of Williams did much to take advantage of the opportunities offered by the Canyon. Several men did a little prospecting, but the town did nothing to connect itself with the Canyon until about 1891. However, once it became aware of the advantages to be gained through such a connection it was more successful than Flagstaff.

The opening of the south rim of the Grand Canyon was a gradual process. In 1885 permanent settlers began to come in. The majority were in search of mineral wealth. The Canyon not only offered riches to the prospectors but also many attractions to the tourist. For the first five years the prospectors and tourists visited the Canyon in small numbers, and through their efforts laid the foundation for the future development of the Canyon. The period from 1885 to 1890 was not one of great achievement, but was rather one of slow and permanent settlement.

---

[47]McClintock, *Arizona*, Vol. II, p. 558.

[48]Bass, *op. cit.*, pp. 36-37.

[49]Noble, L. F., *The Shinumo Quadrangle*, pp. 11-12.

CHAPTER III   MINING AT GRAND CANYON

Prospectors

Grand Canyon owes its early development to prospectors and mining companies. The deposit of minerals within the walls offered the chief inducement to settlers. The latter did not move to the Canyon in large numbers because the minerals were difficult of access. The arduous labor required to extract the ore eliminated the possibility of making large fortunes in a short time. Therefore, the Canyon never experienced a great boom. The men who prospected within her towering walls came chiefly from Flagstaff and Williams and other neighboring towns. Very few of them took up permanent residences. For the most part, they were men with homes elsewhere, who spent their free time, mostly in the winter, prospecting.

There were three main areas along the Canyon's rim where the prospectors concentrated their activities. As mentioned in the preceding chapter, there were two trails, the Tanner and the Hance trails, at the eastern end of the Canyon. The Tanner Trail did not figure prominently in the development of the Canyon, whereas the Hance Trail did. This latter was located about sixteen miles east of the present village of Grand Canyon, Arizona.

The second and most important center of activity was located where Grand Canyon Village stands today. Here Bright Angel Trail begins.[50] The third point of interest along the Canyon's rim was the Bass Camp, located twenty-five miles west of Bright Angel Trail.

Although the Hance and Bass trails were built earlier (1884 and 1889) than the Grand View and Bright Angel Trails, these latter quickly became their rivals for activity, and overshadowed them in importance.

In 1891 William Henry Ashurst, John Marshall, C. H. McClure and Thomas Frier built the Grand View Trail.[51] These men had been prospecting in the Canyon for about four years. They had located many mines which showed signs of rich mineral content. In order to work them it was necessary to build a trail over which they might pack in their equipment and carry out the ore.

That same year work was begun on the Bright Angel Trail. Niles J. Cameron, Peter D. Berry, Robert Ferguson and C. H. McClure constructed it for the

---

[50]Bright Angel is the name applied to this trail, to the Fred Harvey hotel at the head of the trail, to the creek emptying into the river at the foot of the Kaibab trail, to the canyon through which the creek runs and to a point on the north rim overlooking the Bright Angel Canyon. This name originated with J. W. Powell. Major Powell on his river voyage in 1869 named the creek mentioned above, Bright Angel, in contrast to a very muddy one he had passed farther upstream. The latter he called the Dirty Devil. (Ed. Note: Stanton says that Powell named the Dirty Devil after William Dunn, who he had grown to dislike. See "Colorado River Controversies", by R. B. Stanton.)

[51]*Coconino Sun*, June 20, 1891.

development of their mines. They filed it as a toll road,[52] a fact which later caused trouble.

Mining Companies

While the local prospectors were exploring the Canyon, locating claims and building trails, a railroad survey party from Denver, Colorado, went through the Canyon on the river. This was the Robert Brewster Stanton expedition referred to in the first chapter.[53] This expedition gave unexpected impetus to interest in mining in Grand Canyon.[54] Stanton's report of mineral deposits found during the survey were widely circulated. His glowing reports advertised a comparatively unknown region. As a result, mining activities increased and were undertaken on a large scale. Outside companies and capital began to come in, bringing the Grand Canyon into prominence.

The first of the companies to enter the mining field at the Canyon after the Stanton expedition, was the Colorado Grand Canyon Mining and Improvement Company[55] of Denver. This company's stated purposes were: the operation of mines along the Canyon, located by the Stanton expedition, the location of new claims, the establishment of toll roads and a ferry across the river, the operation of hotels on the rim, and the acquisition and sale of real estate.[56]

The company was not very long-lived. Like pioneers in most fields of endeavor, it attempted too much. Mention is here made of it, not because of any great success, but because it was the first of a large number of similar enterprises. Its fate was the rule rather than the exception. The possibility of fabulous riches to be uncovered led many men to organize companies to try their luck. But the Canyon offered unusual obstacles. Obstacles practically impossible to overcome with the equipment on hand at that date. Most companies found that mine development under such great difficulties eliminated all hope of profit. Nevertheless, it required many years' experience to convince them that the Grand Canyon was not the treasure house they had dreamed it to be.

During these years the population at Grand Canyon grew rapidly. The companies, in their vain attempts to keep going, did much toward the development of the area as it is today. Perhaps the greatest benefit it received from them was the railroad.

Flagstaff and Williams saw the advantage of a railroad to Grand Canyon. They both desired it, realizing the tourist trade would be stimulated. Flagstaff lost the railroad for two reasons. She endeavored to persuade railroad companies to put in a

---

[52]*Files of Civil Cases, District Court of the Fourth Judicial District of the Territory of Arizona, in and for the County of Coconino, Case 641*, "Answer of Defense", MS, County Court House, Flagstaff, Arizona.

[53]See above Chapter I, p. 8.

[54]*Coconino Sun*, June 13, 1891.

[55]Ibid., June 13, 1891.

[56]*Record of Articles of Incorporation, Coconino County, Territory of Arizona*, Vol. I, pp. 8-9, Recorder's office, Flagstaff, Arizona.

line chiefly for tourist trade. This trade was not yet large enough to warrant such an expensive undertaking. Besides this, all Flagstaff offered was moral support and what financial aid her wealthier citizens were willing to contribute.

Williams' efforts were more practical. She went to the mining companies, emphasizing the advantage to them of having a means of transportation for their operations. They deeded this transportation and were only too glad of an opportunity to get it. Williams pointed out that in addition, they could carry passengers, which would give them extra revenue. As a final inducement Williams offered a substantial cash subsidy, not just a vague promise as Flagstaff had given.[57]

William Owen ("Buckey") O'Neill, a mine promoter from Prescott, Arizona, started to work to find a company which would build a railroad from Williams.[58] He succeeded in interesting the Lombard, Goode and Company, an eastern firm engaged in mining operations about twenty miles south of the rim.

On July 31, 1897, Lombard, Goode and Company incorporated the Santa Fe and Grand Canyon Railroad Company. Their stated purpose was the construction of a railroad and telegraph line from a point near Williams to the Grand Canyon.[59] The project was started during the first week of March 1898. Although there were great preparations and enthusiasm in Williams, Flagstaff was skeptical, as shown by a clipping in the March 5th issue of the Coconino Sun:

> The building of the Santa Fe and Grand Canyon Railroad was commenced at Williams this week and it is hoped that the project may be finished. But as so many roads have been started in the direction of the Grand Canyon and abandoned after considerable work was done the Sun has serious doubts about a railroad being constructed to the Grand Canyon in this generation.[60]

Before the railroad could be completed, an act of Congress was necessary. In 1893 President Benjamin Harrison, by proclamation, had created the Grand Canyon Forest Reserve, closing the area to entry. The bill authorizing the construction of the railroad was introduced by Delegate Marcus A. Smith of Arizona, and passed by congress, May 18, 1898. This act stated in part:

> Be it enacted... that the Santa Fe and Grand Canyon Railroad company... is authorized to construct and maintain a railroad over and through the Grand Canyon National Forest Reserve... running in a northerly direction from Williams, Arizona; thence proceeding by the most practicable route through a point at or near Lombard and the Bright Angel Trail... in an

[57]McClintock, *Arizona*, Vol. I, p. 295.

[58]Cameron, R. H., "The Bright Angel Trail", *Speeches of Hon. Ralph H. Cameron of Arizona in the Senate of the United States*, p. 21.

[59]*Record of Articles of Incorporation, Coconino County, Territory of Arizona*, Vol. I pp. 123-217, MS, County Recorder's Office, Flagstaff, Arizona.

[60]*Coconino Sun*, March 5, 1898.

easterly direction to the Little Colorado River; also to proceed by such side tracks, extensions, switches and spurs, as may be necessary to reach the various groups of mines in said forest reserve, all in said Coconino County...[61]

Work continued on the Grand Canyon Railroad from 1898 to 1900 under Lombard, Goode and Company. By 1900 production at the Anita mines had ceased. The company had borrowed money to build the railroad, anticipating a rich out-put of ore. When the ore failed to materialize the primary reason for building the railroad ceased to exist, and there were no prospects of the company's paying the debts incurred in the line's construction. In the summer of that year an application for a receivership of the railroad and also for an injunction restraining the parties in possession from incurring further indebtedness in its management, was made.[62] On June 8, 1901, a judgment and decree of foreclosure and sale was made. There was only one bid made at the sale, that of Edward D. Kenna, Byron L. Smith and James H. Eckles, agents for the Santa Fe Railroad Company. Their bid of $150,000.00[63] was made and accepted. On August 10, 1901, they incorporated as the Grand Canyon Railway Company, and turned the company over to the Santa Fe.

While Lombard, Goode and Company were having all their trouble, mining activity continued in other parts. The number of men and companies thus engaged was slowly dwindling, but those who continued, were very active for nearly ten years longer.

Although John Hance had sold his hotel and trail to J. W. Thurber and J. H. Tolfree in 1895, he continued to live at Grand Canyon. He had several mines in the Canyon, the best of which were his asbestos mines discovered in 1892 near the Colorado River at the foot of his trail. There were sixteen of these claims containing a very high grade of asbestos. They were patented in 1901.[64] The same year he bonded them to a company called the Hance Asbestos Mining Company. This was a Massachusetts company headed by George E. Hills. A few months later the company bought the mines for $6,250.00, and appointed Hance superintendent of them. However, the company never did much developing of its property and in 1904 Hance's appointment was revoked. The mines were later sold for taxes, and are still privately owned.[65]

The Last Chance mining claim, in the Canyon below Grand View Point, was located in 1890 by R. A. Ferguson, Peter D. Berry, E. I. Gale, Niles J. Cameron and Thomas McMillan. This mine contained some very rich copper ore, which took first prize for richness at the Chicago World's Fair in 1898.

There were several other mines in this vicinity located three years later. By 1900 they had all been acquired by R. H. Cameron and Peter D. Berry, who had also secured

---

[61] *Statues at Large of the United States of America*, Vol. XXX, Chapter 343, p. 418.

[62]*Coconino Sun*, August 18, 1900.

[63]Austin, *op. cit.*, p.38.

[64]*Record of Deeds*, No. 32, p. 599, County Recorder's Office, Flagstaff, Arizona.

[65]Gilliland, R. P., *Personal Interview*, March 21, 1940.

possession of the Last Chance mine. This group of mines is a good example of what happened to most of the mines at the Grand Canyon. Any financial gains which the owners made were not due to minerals extracted from them, but rather to their sale. This statement is demonstrated by the history of the Cameron-Berry mines. They were located between 1890 and 1893. In 1901 the owners sold them to Henry P. Barbour for $1,875.00. Barbour sold them the same year to R. W. Foster for a recorded sum of $40,000.00. Then in 1902 Foster turned them over to the Canyon Copper Company of which he was a member.[66] In 1913 the Canyon Copper Company sold the mill site to William Randolph Hearst for $25,000.00 and the point and the mines in 1927 for $60,000.00.[67]

Although this outline gives an idea of profit in Grand Canyon mines, very few others ran into such high figures. Their location was the greatest asset to this group of mines. There was not only a good trail leading directly to the mines, but the mill site on the rim commanded one of the finest views of the Canyon. This fact was its greatest advantage after 1902 when tourist travel began to take on greater importance.

Most mines less fortunately situated, never benefited their owners financially. There were over a hundred of these. They were generally permitted to lapse as they were not worth the taxes assessed on them.

As a whole, mining at Grand Canyon never proved to be very profitable to those engaged in it. Nevertheless, it was of inestimable value to the opening and development of the Grand Canyon into the wonderful tourist resort it is today.

Before closing this chapter, mention should be made of one more plan by which it was hoped wealth could be wrested from the Grand Canyon. Many of the early mining companies had conceived the idea of harnessing the Colorado River and converting its strength into electric power to operate the mines. This plan was never put into operation by any of these companies. It was however, tried in 1902 by a commercial electric company, the Grand Canyon Electric Power Company, which had been incorporated on August 23rd of that year by Julius Aubineau, David Babbitt and A. Barman.[68]

Their plan was to generate electricity by utilizing the Bright Angel Creek, a tributary of the Colorado River. The electricity thus generated was to be distributed to Flagstaff and neighboring towns.

Work on the project continued for about two years. At the end of this time the company dissolved for lack of funds.[69] Its members either did not appreciate the tremendous expense of equipment and its installation, or they were disappointed in

---

[66]Other members were; John H. Page, J. G. Verkamp, G. H. Verkamp, J. B. Verkamp, Babbitt Brothers, Harry H. Smith, F. A. Day, Dr. T. M. Prudden, Hon. Carroll S. Page, and James M. Goulding. John H. Page to Peggy Verkamp, April 15, 1940, Phoenix, Arizona.

[67]*Abstract of Title*, No. 1101, Coconino Abstract Company, Flagstaff, Arizona.

[68]*Record of Articles of Incorporation, Coconino County, Territory of Arizona*, Book 1, p. 430, County Recorder's Office, Flagstaff, Arizona.

[69]Babbitt, C. J., *Personal Interview*, March 1, 1940.

financial aid they had counted on receiving. It was just another in a long line of disappointments which were the sole result of expended energy and money.

All these early pioneers left few visible traces to show where they had tampered with the Grand Canyon. A small prospector's hole here and there and a few pieces of decaying and rusted equipment hidden by the bushes and undergrowth of the passing years are all there is to indicate that men have visited and worked along its walls and floor.

CHAPTER IV   TOURIST TRAVEL AT GRAND CANYON

Today the Grand Canyon of the Colorado River is known the world over as a great tourist attraction. The nature lover and the natural scientist are attracted by the wonderful opportunity it offers each for enjoyment and study. There is no longer any interest in its mineral riches. The years of prospecting demonstrated effectively that these minerals are not a source of wealth. Activity in this field had practically ceased even before the United States government stepped in and put a stop to all future prospecting.

Early Stage Lines

The Atlantic and Pacific Railroad was the first to use the Canyon as a commercial asset. When their line was completed to California in 1883, it approached at one point within twenty-five miles of the Canyon's rim. From this point, Peach Springs, Arizona, stages were run to the Canyon. The terminus of the stage line was west of the boundary of the national park. The view of the Canyon from here is considered inferior to that from points within the Park area. Nevertheless, this route continued to be used until about 1901, because it was an all year route. After the railroad was built to the head of the Bright Angel Trail it was abandoned.

The citizens of Flagstaff were anxious to capitalize on the scenic attractions of the Canyon. They had made several unsuccessful attempts to build a railroad to it. Finally, in 1892, the Flagstaff Board of Trade sent a committee to T. R. Gabel, superintendent of the Atlantic and Pacific Railroad to discuss the organization of a stage line leading from that town to the Grand Canyon. Upon the favorable report of the committee, a stock company was formed to build necessary hotels at the half-way point and at the Canyon. Enough stock was taken to build accommodation for fifty visitors.[70] These efforts were a success. In the third week of May, 1892, the stage line and tourist accommodations were opened for business.[71]

The trip was made in one day with three stations, or stops, along the way where passengers rested and obtained refreshments while a change of horses was made. These stations were Little Springs, sixteen miles northwest of Flagstaff on the western slope of the San Francisco Peaks, Cedar Station, eighteen miles farther on in the flats north of the Peaks and Moqui Station, twenty miles north of Cedar.[72] Stages left Flagstaff on Mondays, Wednesdays and Fridays.[73] The fare to Grand Canyon from Flagstaff was twenty dollars.

---

[70]Austin, *op. cit.*, p. 16.

[71]The officers of this company were: President, Dr. P. J. Brannen; Treasurer, J. H. Haskins; Secretary, H. D. Ross; Directors, George Babbitt, Timothy A. Riordan and P. J. Brannen. Management of the hotels was given to I. Chrisman and of the stage line to E. S. Wilcox.

[72]Woods, G. K., *Personal Impression of Grand Canyon*, pp. 23-24.

[73]*Coconino Sun*, September 5, 1891.

This stage company, which was actually controlled by the Atlantic and Pacific Railroad, used the Hance Hotel at the Canyon for its guests until 1895. That year, through its agents, J. W. Thurber and J. H. Tolfree, it bought all Hance's rights to his trail and hotel. Hance received $1,500.00, and agreed not to open another trail or act as guide at any point up or down the Canyon for a distance of thirty miles from the Grand Canyon Hotel.[74]

It is interesting to note in connection with transportation to the Canyon, that as early as 1896 men were riding bicycles over the distance of seventy odd miles. The young men of Flagstaff formed the Coconino Cycling Club, which made an annual run to the Canyon. The trip was made in one day over rough and hilly roads.[75] There were only four of these annual trips, because so few participated. It was too strenuous for most cyclists.

Besides the stages running out of Peach Springs and Flagstaff, there was one out of Williams, which started operating in 1891, the year before the regular one was organized in Flagstaff. W. W. Bass laid out the route and established the stage line which started functioning in the fall of 1891.[76] This route terminated near the present Grand Canyon Village. The following year the stage line was run by Sanford Rowe, a livery man from Williams. Bass then started a second line from Ash Fork, Arizona, which led to his camp.

For the next eight years stage coaches continued to be the only means of transport for Grand Canyon visitors. It was not until 1899 that a railroad finally approached its rim. Under the original company, this railroad only reached Anita, a mining camp twenty-one miles south of the rim. Train tourists were met at Anita by stages and driven to the head of Bright Angel Trail, where the Santa Fe and Grand Canyon Railroad maintained a hotel, under the direction of the Atlantic and Pacific Railroad. The latter company had loaned the money for the construction of the hotel.[77]

After acquiring the Grand Canyon Railroad in 1901, the Santa Fe completed the line to the Canyon's rim, where on September 19, the first train arrived.

Hotels at Grand Canyon

During the first part of September, 1901, the Santa Fe surveyed the boundaries for the station grounds. It had been allotted the usual twenty acres as specified in the act of 1875, granting railroads the right of way through public lands.[78] Plans were immediately begun for the erection of tourist accommodations within the surveyed

[74]*Coconino Sun*, November 7, 1895.

[75]Austin, *op.cit.*, pp. 30-31.

[76]*Coconino Sun*, September 5, 1891.

[77]*Files of Civil Cases, District Court of the Fourth Judicial District of the Territory of Arizona, in and for the County of Coconino*, Case 725, "Direct Examination of R.B. Burns", County Court House, Flagstaff, Arizona.

[78]*Statutes at Large of the United States of America*, Vol. XVIII, Chapter 152, p. 482.

boundaries. A log cabin which was serving as a hotel was added to and tent cabins built around it. It was named Bright Angel Camp.

In 1902 plans were begun for a new hotel to be built a little east of the Bright Angel Camp. In October 1903, construction was started. The management of the hotel was given to the Fred Harvey Company. This latter company had been in charge of all the eating houses along the Santa Fe from Albuquerque, New Mexico, to Barstow, California, since 1897.[79] With the addition of the hotel at Grand Canyon, the Fred Harvey Company had control of the entire system from Kansas City, Missouri, to Barstow.

The hotel was opened to the public on January 14, 1905.[80] It was named El Tovar after one of the Spanish Conquistadors, who was a member of Coronado's expedition of 1540. That this man's name should have been used seems strange. He never saw the Grand Canyon.[81]

The transfer of the Grand Canyon Railway from Lombard, Goode and Company to the Santa Fe created a question regarding taxation. In 1905 Coconino County assessed the two Harvey hotels at the Canyon and the following year the railroad itself.[82] The railroad objected, claiming tax exemption for itself and the hotels by virtue of Act 68, Section 1, passed by the territorial Legislature on May 16, 1899, which said in part:

> (All property) used or necessary in the construction and operation of railroads..., and whether owned or operated by a person, or persons, association or railway corporation, his heirs or its successors or asigns (sic), be and the same is hereby declared to be exempt from any and all manner of taxation for and during the period of ten years from and after the date of the passage of this act.[83]

The assessment had been made by the county on the advice of E. M. Doe, a Flagstaff lawyer. Doe advanced the view that, while the Santa Fe and Grand Canyon Railroad Company was entitled to exemption, the present owners could only acquire the right to purchase and operate the railroad. The original company's exemption did not inure to the Santa Fe, according to his theory.[84]

With the assessment of the taxes on the hotels and the railroad mileage the Santa Fe brought suit against the county claiming it did not have to pay the taxes. The railroad was defeated in the district court. The case was appealed and went to the

---

[79]*Arizona Champion*, April 23, 1887.

[80]*Files of Civil Cases, District Court of the Fourth Judicial District of the Territory of Arizona, in and for the County of Coconino*, Case 725, "Direct Examination of R. B. Burns", MS, County Court House, Flagstaff, Arizona.

[81]See above Chapter I, p.2.

[82]*Coconino Sun*, June 17, 1906.

[83]*Session Laws of the Twentieth Legislative Assembly of the Territory of Arizona*, Act 68, p.79.

[84]*Coconino Sun*, June 17, 1906.

Supreme Court of Arizona. The Supreme Court reversed the decision of the lower court holding: "that such act (Act 68 of the Twentieth Legislature)[85] perpetuated the exemption unto the successors of the original owner of a railroad constructed pursuant to the act."[86] As a result of this decision, the railroad deferred paying taxes into the county treasury until May, 1909, when the period of exemption ended.

The opening of the hotels by the railroad did not immediately affect the older hotels. They continued to serve the public for nearly ten years longer. The stage line from Flagstaff carried many visitors to the Canyon after the opening of the railroad. The majority of the stage patrons stayed at one of the three hotels at the eastern end of the Canyon. Of these three, mention has already been made of the Hance Hotel. This was the first. The second was a log cabin on the Last Chance mill site. This one was run by P. D. Berry, one of the miners who built the Grand View Trail. Berry did not depend entirely upon the Flagstaff tourist, but also got many train travelers. In 1900, while the train terminus was still at Anita, he ran a stage from this point to his hotel.[87]

In 1902 the Canyon Copper Company bought the Cameron-Berry mining claims, among them the Last Chance mine and mill site. This company had been formed that year by John H. Page. The Canyon Copper Company continued to use Berry's original log cabin as a hotel and in 1903 they added sixty rooms to it. Berry, after the sale of his mining property, homesteaded a new location directly south of the Grand View Hotel.[88] Here he built another cabin, which, with some tents, he ran as tourist accommodations. This establishment he called Summit.

Besides these three hotels or camps, there were still two others not connected with the railroad. One of these, Cameron's hotel, was built very close to the Bright Angel Hotel. It was owned by Ralph H. Cameron, the best known of all the early Grand Canyon residents. His story will be told in the following chapter.

Cameron kept his hotel open until 1910 when he was elected delegate from Arizona to the United States Congress. During the period this hotel was in existence it was the center of much dissension. The railroad disliked the competition it offered the Bright Angel Hotel. In order to make it less accessible to train passengers, the station was moved about a thousand feet to the east. Although this was much more inconvenient for the tourist, it insured their passing the Bright Angel Hotel before seeing Cameron's.[89]

The only other tourist hotel was Bass Camp. By 1902 Bass was well equipped to take care of the increase in the number of his guests, which resulted from the coming of the railroad. He catered to hunting and prospecting parties. To accommodate these parties and also to work his copper and asbestos mines, Bass had constructed a trail from his camp to the north rim. This trail he named Mystic Spring Trail. In order to

---

[85]See Above.

[86]*Reports of Cases Argued and Determined in the Supreme Court of the Territory of Arizona*, Civil Case 1032. Vol. XII. p. 70.

[87]*Coconino Sun*, July 28, 1900.

[88]Page, J. H., *Personal Interview*, March 18, 1940.

[89]Kolb, E., *Personal Interview*, April 13, 1940.

reach the north rim, parties using this trail were ferried across the river from the foot of the trail to the mouth of Shinumo Canyon. Through this little side canyon the trail continued, ascending the steep walls until it finally terminated on the Kaibab Plateau or north rim.

In the Shinumo Canyon, Bass cultivated a small fruit and vegetable garden by means of irrigation. In season, fruit and vegetables were packed out to the camp. Guests could then enjoy the unusual experience of eating fresh fruits and vegetables in this out-of-the-way place.[90]

Four miles southwest of Grand Canyon Village the trains made a stop at a point called Bass. Here W. W. Bass met his guests with a stage and drove them overland twenty-five miles to his camp, which could also be reached by roads from either Ash Fork or Williams. Bass owned the camp until December 11, 1925, when he sold it to the Santa Fe Land and Improvement Company for $20,500.00[91] This property is still assessed to the Santa Fe.

The ever increasing tourist travel to the Grand Canyon opened up two new lines of business; namely, the sale of souvenirs and photography. The first curio store for Canyon tourists was started in 1894 in the Grand Canyon stage line office in Flagstaff.[92]

Curios and Photography

The first curios at Grand Canyon were brought up from Flagstaff to the Canyon by J. G. Verkamp for Babbitt Brothers Trading Company. Verkamp rented one of the Bright Angel tents as his display room. However, business was slow and after a few weeks the stock was sold to Martin Buggeln, the proprietor of Bright Angel Hotel.[93]

The Fred Harvey Company entered the curio business in 1905. That year El Tovar Hotel and the Hopi House were completed. The latter was the Harvey company's curio shop, the first building to be constructed for this particular kind of business.

J. G. Verkamp returned to the Grand Canyon in 1905 to construct a building a little east of the Hopi House. Here he went into the curio business for himself. The store was opened in January, 1906.

The curio business proved a profitable one, thanks to the tourists' insatiable desire to possess souvenirs of their travels. They must also have pictures of the places they visit. The Kolb Brothers of Pittsburgh, Pennsylvania, saw in this the opportunity of establishing a photographic studio.

In 1903 Emery and Ellsworth Kolb started work in this field. They too started in a tent, with a finishing room in the Canyon at Indian Gardens. These two men did not confine themselves entirely to the photographic work. They spent many years exploring canyons and walls of the Grand Canyon before unknown. Their crowning

[90]Lauzon, H., *Personal Interview*, March 22, 1940.

[91]*Record of Deeds*, Book 55, pp. 121-124, County Recorder's Office, Flagstaff, Arizona.

[92]*Coconino Sun*, June 7, 1894.

[93]Verkamp, J. G., *Personal Interview*, April 11, 1940.

achievement was the navigation of the Colorado River from Wyoming to the Gulf of California in 1911. They were the first to cover this entire distance in one trip.

Although they made the trip from a love of adventure, the Kolb brothers did not overlook the commercial possibilities. They went equipped with cameras, still and movie, and films. They made a pictorial record of their trip which has been shown to thousands since.

In 1912 the Kolb brothers made an extensive tour through the large cities of the country, showing their pictures.[94] This tour was of great value to the Grand Canyon, by bringing it to the attention of the American public in such a realistic manner.

The events followed so far have pertained entirely to the south rim of the Grand Canyon. It was on this rim that the first white men discovered it and the first settlers located. The north rim had virtually no contact with the outer world. It belonged to Arizona, but was neglected, because it was practically inaccessible. Arizona's energies were entirely directed toward the development of the south rim.

A few men had seen the Canyon from the north rim and found signs of minerals. In 1902 John Cram and Royal Wolley of Kanab, Utah, and S. Cobb of Boston, found a fissure vein on Point Sublime, directly across the Canyon from Bass Camp.[95] Not much work was ever done on this claim which they located, because it was so remote from refining facilities. It was allowed to lapse shortly after its location.

North Rim

The country north of the Grand Canyon was used to some extent for grazing. There was a great deal of wild game there too. This drew hunting parties, who approached the region from either the south rim or Utah. The great virgin forest was attractive to lumbermen. In 1909 a company from Fredonia, Arizona, attempted to build a railroad into this forest, both for lumbering purposes and tourist travel.[96] Delegate Ralph Cameron tried to secure government aid for the project, but was not successful.[97] The railroad never became a reality.

In 1913 E. D. Woolley of Kanab, Utah, tried to interest his state and Arizona in building an automobile road to the north rim of the Canyon.[98] He received no co-operation from Arizona as the towns and counties along the northern route of the ocean to ocean highway fought the matter. They did not wish any of the tourist travel to be diverted up through Utah. Finally, in 1915, Woolley took matters into his own hands and inaugurated an automobile stage line from Lund, Utah, a station on the Salt Lake Railroad route.[99]

The year 1884 saw the beginning of tourist travel to the Canyon and brought to the attention of many people the great possibilities of such a trend. However, the

---

[94]Kolb , E., *Personal Interview*, March 18, 1940.

[95]*Coconino Sun*, November 22, 1902.

[96]*Coconino Sun*, November 26, 1909.

[97]Ibid., August 6, 1909.

[98]Ibid., July 25, 1913.

[99]Ibid., February 19, 1915.

early mining activity overshadowed it in importance for twenty years. But it continued to grow steadily, until now it is the only permanent source of business at the Canyon.

CHAPTER V   THE BRIGHT ANGEL TRAIL

Controversies Over Toll Collection

Nothing at the Grand Canyon caused as much bitter controversy between the citizens of Coconino County and the railroad, and the county and the Federal Government as did the Bright Angel Trail. The conflict over this trail was carried on from 1901 until 1928, creating hard feelings and mistrust on all sides.

The trouble began in April, 1903, when Ralph Cameron notified Martin Buggeln that the Bright Angel Trail belonged to him and his associates, and they were going to charge toll for all animals passing over it. Buggeln at the time was the proprietor of the Bright Angel Hotel. He had a contract with the Grand Canyon Railway Company, by which he paid no set sum as rent for his location on the station grounds, but a percentage of his receipts from the hotel, curios and horses. His contract granted him the right to hire guides and keep horses for his guests.

From 1901, when he bought the Bright Angel Hotel from J. W. Thurber,[100] until he received Cameron's notice, he had been using the trail free of charge. The owners had not been collecting toll from anyone, not because they did not want to, but because the Secretary of the Interior had threatened to prosecute anyone operating the Bright Angel Trail as a toll road.

In January, 1903, Ralph Cameron received notice through Forest Supervisor S. R. Breen, that his application for exclusive use of the Bright Angel Trail had been granted by the Secretary of the Interior, thus removing the previous threat.[101] It was then that he notified Buggeln that tolls would be collected in the future.

On May 1, Martin Buggeln secured an injunction restraining Cameron from the use of the trail.[102] The issue was immediately taken to court for Buggeln by the railroad's lawyers. His claim was that Cameron never owned the trail or the franchise to collect tolls.

As the case proceeded it developed that the trail had been started in 1891 by Niles J. Cameron, P. D. Berry, Robert Ferguson and C. H. McClure. These men had sent P. D. Berry as their representative to Flagstaff to record the trail as a toll road. The following is a copy of the record:

> I, Peter D. Berry, of the town of Flagstaff, County of Yavapai, Territory of Arizona, do hereby certify that I have commenced the construction of and intend to complete a toll road commencing at law (sic) water mark on the Colorado River and a point twenty-six hundred feet west of the mouth of Bright Angel Creek, running thence through the Indian Gardens in the Grand Canyon of the Colorado River and terminating at the rim of said Grand Canyon at a point about fifteen miles west of what is known as the House Trail and about two and one-

---

[100]*Coconino Sun*, June 25, 1901.
[101]*Coconino Sun*, January 10, 1903.
[102]Austin, E., *op. cit.*, p. 62.

half miles northwest of Hull's tank. The said last mentioned terminus of said toll road being designated by a stake marked "Bright Angel Toll Road" and surrounded by a mound of stones. Said toll road shall be known as the Bright Angel Toll Road a plat of which said toll road is hereto annexed.

signed:

Peter D. Berry[103]

By the toll road law of the territory, any man could go on the public domain and build a trail or road. He was allowed to charge tolls on it for ten years. At the expiration of the ten years, if he had not collected the sum of his original investment, the Board of Supervisors of the county in which the trail or road was located had the privilege of extending his franchise for five years longer.[104]

In 1901, when the original franchise expired, the owners of the Bright Angel Trail requested that the Board of Supervisors grant them the five year extension. This was granted on January 31, 1901.[105] It was in that year that Ralph Cameron had begun to buy out the builders of the trail.

The case against Cameron was carried to the Supreme Court of the Territory of Arizona. It was shown by the evidence that the franchise was not in his name. Judge Sloan held that the franchise for a toll road could neither be sold nor assigned.[106] Upon this decision Ralph Cameron turned the trail back to its original owners.

The railroad began immediate proceedings against these men, ordering them to show by what right they claimed the franchise. In December of 1903, the District Court decided in favor of the defendants, but the case was appealed, and not settled definitely until January 10, 1905. At that time the Supreme Court sustained the decision of the District Court.[107]

From May 1, 1903, when the restraining injunction was granted to Buggeln, until December 17, 1903, when the District Court rescinded it, no tolls were collected by the trail owners. Consequently they initiated a suit to force Martin Buggeln to pay them the sum of $3,000.00. They claimed that during the period that the injunction against them was in effect, 3,000 persons has used the trail without paying toll. On September 21, 1906, the District Court decided in their favor, awarding them $2,000.00 to be paid by Buggeln.[108] However, the case was appealed and on May 25, 1907, the decision was reversed and the plaintiffs had to pay the court expenses.

---

[103]*Files of Civil Cases, District Court of The Fourth Judicial District, in and for Coconino County*, Case 729, "Bill of exceptions", MS, p. 39.

[104]Cameron, R., *op. cit.*, p. 13.

[105]*Minutes of the Board of Supervisors*, Coconino County, Vol. II, p. 276.

[106]*Coconino Sun*, May 2, 1907.

[107]*Files of Civil Cases, District Court of the Fourth Judicial District, in and for Coconino County*, Case 729, "Complaint", MS.

[108]*Files of Civil Cases, District Court of the Fourth Judicial District, in and for Coconino County*, Case 641, MS.

One case after another was initiated. A decision was rendered in some, while many were dismissed. All were practically the same, and the results were always the same. The railroad was unable to get control of the trail.

Martin Buggeln withdrew from the fight in 1906, by selling his interest in the Bright Angel Hotel to the Fred Harvey Company. He did not, however, leave the Canyon. On March 11, 1907, he bought the Hance property on the rim of the Canyon for $5,000.00,[109] and ran a cattle ranch there until his death on November 21, 1939.

Coconino County Acquires Possession of the Trail

The trouble over the Bright Angel Trail continued even after 1906, when Coconino County took it over. Ralph Cameron was elected chairman of the Board of Supervisors of Coconino County in 1904. He tried to get that body to renew the franchise, but they refused, stating:

> Whereas, it appeared to the Board that the term of the franchise covering the Bright Angel Toll Road... has expired as to the said owners, and
>
> Whereas, it is by law, made the duty of the Board to either declare that same a free highway or to proceed to maintain the same as a toll road, and
>
> Whereas, in either case the burden of maintaining said road in suitable condition will devolve upon the county, and
>
> Whereas, it is deemed best for the county and public interest the Supervisors should continue the same as a toll road, and
>
> Whereas, L. L. Ferrell[110] has offered to enter into a contract providing for the care and maintenance of said road and collect tolls thereon, he has submitted the following contract, which was adopted by a vote of two to one.[111]

The Railroad's Attempts to Gain Control of the Trail

While the exchange of the Bright Angel Trail was being made from the original owners to the county, the railroad tried a strategic move. It applied to the Bureau of Forestry of the United States for a permit to operate and control the trail. Word of this plan reached the Board of Supervisors, who wired to the Bureau asking that the request be ignored. The sheriff was authorized to protect the trail against anyone attempting to interfere with the county's possession and control.[112]

---

[109]*Record of Deeds*, Book 32, p. 595, County Recorder's Office, Flagstaff, Arizona.

[110](Ed. note: Lannes L. Ferrall)

[111]*Minutes of the Board of Supervisors of Coconino County*, Vol. III, pp. 127-128.

[112]*Minutes of the Board of Supervisors of Coconino County*, Vol. III, pp. 143-144.

Having failed to obtain the requested permit from the Bureau of Forestry, the railroad attacked L. L. Ferrell's contract with the county. This contract stated that Ferrell should maintain the trail in good condition and collect the tolls. In return he was permitted to keep the entire amount collected. In the suit against Ferrell the railroad succeeded in getting Henry Ashurst, the District Attorney for Coconino County, to lend his name. When the case came up Ferrell's attorneys claimed that the court could not decide Ferrell's rights unless the county was made a defendant, because he was only the county's agent, under a five year contract. The court agreed, and Ashurst had to bring suit against the county, whose attorney he was.[113]

The complaint in this case was the same as that of practically all the former cases. The plaintiff claimed the defendants, L. L. Ferrell and the County of Coconino, had no right, authority or warrant of law to use, hold or exercise the franchise to collect tolls on the Bright Angel Trail.

While this case was being tried, Ralph Cameron, went to Phoenix to the legislature and had a bill passed which was called the Cameron Bill. This bill (Council Bill 77) stated that:

> Upon the expiration or forfeiture of any toll road franchise, the ownership with all rights and privileges, shall vest in the county... in which it is located... the Board of Supervisors of the county in which such road may be situated, shall have the power to make and enter into a contract with some person or persons upon such terms as shall be agreed upon whereby such person or persons shall have the control and management of such toll-road...[114]

This bill passed both houses, but was vetoed by Governor Kibbey, because of a telegram he received from the Secretary of the Interior, E. A. Hitchcock, saying:

> I am advised that the Territorial Legislature has passed a bill permitting a toll road within the Grand Canyon Forest Reserve. It has been the policy of the administration to extinguish and refuse such privileges, and the public interests demand that I shall call this matter to your attention for your consideration, as to whether or not such a measure, not in harmony with the policy of the administration should become law.[115]

The bill was passed unanimously over the governor's veto.

The county now had nothing to worry about. It was in full and undeniable possession of the trail. Ralph Cameron still wanted the trail, and so did the railroad. The county had a contract with Ferrell, but actually wanted Cameron to have it.

---

[113] Austin, E., *op. cit.*, pp. 86-87.

[114] *Acts, Resolutions and Memorials of the Twenty-fourth Legislative Assembly of the Territory of Arizona*, pp. 76-77.

[115] *Coconino Sun*, March 21, 1907.

Ferrell was willing to give up his contract in favor of Cameron. When the railroad heard of the proposed change of contract, it put in a bid, offering the county 70% of the tolls collected. However, this generous offer was ignored as the county had no intention of letting the Santa Fe get its hands on the trail.

At a meeting of the Board of Supervisors on April 17, 1907, the following resolution was passed:

> Be it resolved that the term of the Bright Angel Toll Road franchise, and all the rights and privileges pertaining thereto, shall be... extended for the future... period of five years; and the said Ralph H. Cameron is hereby authorized and empowered to take and resume possession and control of said toll road. Provided that Ralph H. Cameron, his grantees and assignees shall pay to the county of Coconino ten per cent of the tolls collected... Coconino County does hereby surrender to said Ralph H. Cameron possession and control of said toll road...[116]

Although this should have ended the controversy of the Bright Angel Trail, the railroad continued in its efforts to get a courts' decision ousting Cameron from its possession. These cases constituted a continual nuisance, but no serious threat.

The Santa Fe finally built its own trail into the Canyon at the Hermit Basin eight miles west of El Tovar. It was simply an improvement of the old Boucher (Boo-shay) Trail. This trail had been built by Louis Boucher, a sheepman, to some mines he had located in the Canyon. On the plateau level the company constructed a tourist camp. The trail and camp were completed in 1912.[117]

The National Government's Purchase of the Trail

With the creation of the Grand Canyon National Park in 1919, the United States government began negotiations to buy the Bright Angel Trail from the county of Coconino.[118] The first propositions were made through W. H. Peters, National Park Engineer. He attempted high-handed methods with the Board of Supervisors, and greatly antagonized that body. In a letter from the Board to Peters they stated, "that in view of your previous attitude and discourtesy to the members of this body... they do not care to make any proposition to or through you."[119]

Further negotiations were then dropped until 1923. In that year some of the business men of Flagstaff began to urge the sale of the trail to the Federal Government. The Hayden bill creating the park had a section which provided authorization to the Secretary of the Interior "to negotiate with the said county... for

---

[116]*Minutes of the Board of Supervisors, County of Coconino*, Vol. III, pp. 242-243.

[117]*Files of Civil Cases, District Court of the Fourth Judicial District, in and for Coconino County*, Case 962, "Complaint", MS, March 25, 1912.

[118]*Minutes of the Board of Supervisors, Coconino County*, Vol. IV, Book 2, p. 379.

[119]*Minutes of the Board of Supervisors, Coconino County*, Vol. IV, Book 2, p. 397.

the purchase of said Bright Angel Toll Road and Trail and all rights therein..."[120] The business men wanted to sell the trail for $1,000,000.00, to be expended on a road between Maine, Arizona and the south boundary of the park.[121] A temporary agreement was reached, subject to referendum by the voters. The question of the sale of the trail was put on the ballot for the General Election of November 4, 1924. The vote went against the proposal.[122]

Finally, in 1927, state Senator Walter Runke of Flagstaff introduced a bill in the legislature to make the disposal of the Bright Angel Trail easier. It provided that any county owning a toll road in a national park was authorized to sell all rights, title and interest to the United States. The negotiations were to be carried on between the Board of Supervisors and the Secretary of the Interior.[123]

This opened the way for the final sale of the Bright Angel Trail. At a special meeting of the Board of Supervisors, called on October 17, 1927, a letter was sent to the Secretary of the Interior, containing an offer of sale. It said in part:

> In order that the County of Coconino may be relieved from all further expenditures either for construction or maintenance of roads from National Old Trails Highway to south boundary of Grand Canyon National Park, we, the Board of Supervisors agree to sell the Bright Angel Trail to the United States upon receipt of assurances that the Federal Government is willing to commence construction of said approach road.[124]

On May 22, 1928, the deed conveying the Bright Angel Trail to the United States was executed.[125] It provided that the Federal Government should appropriate $1,000,000.00 as the price of the trail. This amount was to be spent by the Government on the construction of an approach road to the south boundary of the Grand Canyon National Park, leading from National Old Trails Highway.

Ralph Cameron fought the sale of the Bright Angel Trail to the bitter end. Many of his motives were personal, but he foresaw that the people of Coconino County would not really benefit by the sale in the long run. He wanted the trail to be paid for in cash, deposited in the county treasury. He knew that the government would have to keep up an approach road to the park regardless of whether or not the sale of the trail was made. He also knew that Congress had already appropriated the money for such a road. The sale of the trail simply saved the Federal Government the money of the first appropriation. The government no longer maintains the approach road, but has turned it over to the State of Arizona. Now the people of Coconino County

---

[120]Tolsen, H. A., *Laws Relating to the National Park Service, The National Parks and Monuments*, pp. 205-209.

[121]*Minutes of the Board of Supervisors of Coconino County*, Vol. V, p. 33.

[122]Warner, A., "Canyons and Camerons", *Nation*, Vol. 121, October 28, 1925.

[123]*Session Laws of the State of Arizona 1927*, Vol. XII, Chapter 26, p. 188.

[124]*Minutes of the Board of Supervisors of Coconino County*, Vol. V, pp. 377-378.

[125]*Record of Deeds*, Book 56, pp. 381-382, County Recorder's Office, Flagstaff, Arizona.

continue to pay for the approach road they thought they received in exchange for the trail.

Ralph Cameron tried to warn the people of this outcome, but he had so many personal interests connected with the trail, they did not realize that his motives were not entirely selfish.

Ralph H. Cameron is the Grand Canyon's most outstanding character. He was born in Southport, Maine, on October 21, 1863. He came to Arizona in 1883 and made his first visit to the Canyon in 1884. He returned in 1887 to prospect and located many mining claims. He was chiefly a promoter and politician and always in the thick of some fight. He was a man of the people and very popular with them. He believed in keeping the state and its resources for the local citizens and did all in his power to keep large companies and the Federal Government from grabbing too much. This desire led him into one controversy after another.

Controversies Over Ralph Cameron's Mining Claims

The Bright Angel Trail was not the only bone of contention which brought him and the Grand Canyon into prominence. His mining claims, which he always seemed to have located in someone's way, were forever causing trouble.

In 1901 the railroad surveyed the twenty acres it was entitled to for the station grounds. A short time later Cameron located two mining claims, the Cape Horn and the Golden Eagle, on approximately the same land. On these claims he built a hotel, livery stables and tent bedrooms.[126]

In 1905 Cameron had these claims surveyed officially and made application for a patent. The railroad contended that the claims in question were not mineral and that the requisite amount of assessment work had not been done. The case came up before Register Hildreth and Receiver Moore. They decided that the railroad had not proved their allegations.[127]

Again in 1906 the case was brought up. The railroad claimed that location notification on these claims had failed to state that the whole or any part of them had located on abandoned property, and that no vein or other deposit of mineral had been disclosed in any of the workings within the boundaries of the claims. The decision in this case was that Cameron had fulfilled all the requirements of the mining laws. But he had located his claims in April, 1902, while the railroad had made their survey for the station grounds the previous year. Therefore, where the claims overlapped one another the railroad held the prior right.[128]

The settlement of the dispute with the railroad did not end Cameron's fight to hold his mining claims. In addition to those on the rim he had located seventeen in the Canyon along the Bright Angel Trail. They were so located as to command the

---

[126]*Files of Civil Cases, District Court of the Fourth Judicial District, in and for Coconino County*, Case 1048, "Defendants' Argument and Brief", MS, pp. 15-16.

[127]*Coconino Sun*, September 30, 1905.

[128]Austin, E., *op. cit.*, p. 77.

greatest possible mileage of that trail.[129]   In 1913 the Government began a series of suits in an attempt to take them from him.   It finally won in 1920, when the question reached the Supreme Court of the United States.   That court decided that Cameron's claims were not valid and therefore, he and his associates were trespassers in the Grand Canyon National Park.

Cameron refused to accept the verdict and continued operating his claims at Indian Gardens in the Canyon.   Attorney General Stone tried very hard to get some action taken to force Cameron to obey the verdict.   Not until 1923 did he succeed.

With the relinquishment of his claims, Cameron's personal connections with the Grand Canyon were severed.   However, his interest in it did not end here.   He continued his political influence until the sale of the Bright Angel Trail.   This was his final stand and with that gone he never again took an active part in events at Grand Canyon.

---

[129]*Files of Civil Cases, District Court of the Fourth Judicial District, in and for Coconino County*, Case 725, "Complaint", MS.

CHAPTER VI   GRAND CANYON NATIONAL PARK

It seems strange that such a great tourist attraction as Grand Canyon, should remain so long without national park status. Yet there were several causes for this. They were chiefly ignorance and local opposition. It required a great deal of effort on the part of the National Government to overcome these, before it could set aside this natural wonder as a national park.

The first proposal for the establishment of Grand Canyon National Park was introduced in 1886 by Benjamin Harrison, then Senator from Indiana.[130] The proposal failed, more for lack of enthusiasm than opposition. In fact, the Flagstaff paper made the following comment at the time; "The National Park of the Grand Cañon of the Colorado sounds well. The National Park of the Grand Cañon of the Colorado will be a Mecca of tourists from all the world over".[131] But the Canyon was too little known or appreciated for the politicians to take the step. The idea of national parks was a comparatively new one. There existed only one national park at this date — Yellowstone National Park, 1872.

Senator Harrison's proposal aroused little attention and no action. He was not to be put off so easily, however. He bided his time, until he was in a position where he could do something about the matter. His chance came when he was elected President of the United States.

Creation of Grand Canyon Forest Reserve

On February 20, 1893, President Harrison issued the proclamation creating the "Great Canyon Reserve" in the northern part of Coconino County.

> I, Benjamin Harrison, President of the United States... do hereby make known and proclaim that there is hereby reserved from entry and settlement and set apart as a Public Reservation, all those certain tracts, pieces or parcels of land lying... within the boundaries... described as follows...[132]
> Excepting from the force and effect of this proclamation all lands which may have been embraced in any legal entry... or upon which any valid settlement has been made pursuant to law..., and all mining claims duly located and held according to the laws of the United States...
> Provided that this exception shall not continue to apply to any particular tract of land unless the entryman, settler or claimant continues to comply with the law...[133]

---

[130]Freeman, L. R., *The Colorado River*, p. 442.

[131]*Arizona Champion*, January 23, 1886.

[132]The south line of the reserve ran just north of the San Francisco Mountains and extended north one degree. The west line was just west of Cataract Canyon and extended east one degree. These lines embraced all the scenic portions of Grand Canyon.

[133]*Statutes at Large of the United States of America*, Vol. XXVII, pp. 1064-65.

By the time of this proclamation a number of men were mining and raising livestock in the region affected by it. They did not welcome the restrictions imposed on them by it and in many cases ignored them. The United States government from this time on was to find that it could not appropriate to itself a section of Arizona without opposition from the inhabitants. As the population increased and the wealth of the country was realized the opposition grew stronger. The pioneer was not interested in the benefit to be derived by the nation as a whole from government ownership of this new land. His sole interest was his own establishment there. Any government activity of this sort was an interference not to be appreciated, and to be actively opposed when it grew too strong.

The National Government was not the only one with designs on the Grand Canyon. Arizona's northern neighbor, Utah, made many attempts to get possession of the north rim of the Canyon. As early as 1896 Utah's Legislature suggested annexing this area,[134] proposing the Colorado River as the boundary between the two territories. As no action could be taken without the concurrence of Arizona the proposal failed. The latter had no intention of relinquishing any of its territory so easily. Utah even attempted to have an act passed by the Congress of the United States in 1902, granting her the Colorado River as her southern boundary. But these and all similar attempts failed.

The constant protesting against the Proclamation of 1893 led the Coconino County Board of Supervisors to pass the following resolution. On June 11, 1898, that body unanimously resolved:

> that any measure or movement, either on the part of the President or of the Congress of the United States to restore to the public domain all or any part of said forest reserve by and the same is hereby most earnestly approved and commended by this Board; and be it further resolved, that the co-operation of the Board with any movement looking toward the restoration of said reserve or any part thereof to the public domain, is hereby most heartily pledged.[135]

In spite of this weighty indication of the sentiments of the people of Coconino County, another movement toward the creation of the Grand Canyon National Park was started that same year. The local paper pointed out the potent sources of opposition, trying at the same time to quiet the fears of the miners by saying, "It is reasonable to suppose, however, that Uncle Sam has no disposition to leave his hidden wealth lie dormant, and that the mining laws will apply there as elsewhere".[136]

However, this second proposal received so much opposition and so little support, it made scant progress, and was early abandoned. The question was then dropped for ten years, though not forgotten.

---

[134]Austin, E., *op. cit.*, p. 28.

[135]*Minutes of the Board of Supervisors, Coconino County,* Vol. II, p. 105.

[136]*Coconino Sun*, September 24, 1898.

May 6, 1903, President Theodore Roosevelt visited the Grand Canyon.[137] People from the entire territory of Arizona went to the Canyon to welcome him. Amid the cheers of a crowd of about eight hundred Arizonians he mounted a white horse and rode out to the Grand Canyon Hotel, sixteen miles east of the depot. He dined with John H. Page at Grand View, where he was served regular miner's fare.

Creation of Grand Canyon National Monument

Roosevelt was much impressed by the Canyon. He found on its rim a thriving little community. A post office had been established in 1902 with Martin Buggeln as postmaster. There were two voting precincts.[138] It was no longer isolated as it had been for so many years. But in spite of the progress made here toward organized community life, Roosevelt's attention was called to the fact that there still was a great deal of disorder. The quarrels over the Bright Angel Trail and over the Cape Horn and Golden Eagle mining claims were well under way. Men carried guns wherever they went, and the population was well divided into two camps, the railroad and its adherents versus the miners and theirs.

This state of affairs was doing serious harm to the development of the Grand Canyon. President Roosevelt realizing this made an attempt to put it under Government control. One of his last acts as President of the United States was the issuance on January 11, 1908, of a proclamation creating Grand Canyon National Monument.

> I, Theodore Roosevelt President of the United States of America... do proclaim that there is hereby reserved from appropriation and use of all kinds under all the public land laws, subject to all prior valid adverse claims, and set apart as a National Monument, all the tracts of land in the Territory of Arizona, shown as the Grand Canyon National Monument on the diagram forming a part hereof.
>
> The reservation made by this proclamation is not intended to prevent the use of the lands for forest purposes under the proclamation establishing the Grand Canyon National Forest, not the two reservations shall both be effective on the land withdrawn...
>
> Warning is hereby given to all unauthorized persons not to appropriate, injure or destroy any feature of this National Monument or to locate or settle upon any of the lands reserved by the proclamation.[139]

This move did little to improve conditions at the Canyon because the administration of national monuments was anything but systematic. Some were under the jurisdiction of the War Department and some under that of the Department

---

[137]McClintock, *Arizona*, Vol. II, p. 543.

[138]The first was at the head of Bright Angel Trail, the other at Grand View Hotel.

[139]*Statutes at Large of the United States of America*, Vol. XXXV, pp. 2175-2176.

of the Interior. The Grand Canyon National Monument was given to this latter department, and handled as an incidental item by it.

President Roosevelt's interest in the Canyon was genuine. His efforts to improve it failed only because he lacked governmental equipment to do what he knew needed to be done. He visited the Canyon twice after leaving office. The last time he went to the north rim hunting.

The work of preserving the Grand Canyon for the immediate and future enjoyment of the nation had to be done by individual men. The Canyon had not yet grown to the point where Congress felt it important enough to command their attention. President Harrison and President Roosevelt had used their power of issuing proclamations to try to protect it. President Taft[140] included the Grand Canyon National Monument in the Grand Canyon game reserve.

In 1909 Secretary of the Interior Ballinger, in his annual report stated:

> The Grand Canyon of the Colorado was established as a national monument on January 11, 1908. Its status is not such as would authorize the granting of concessions or of controlling travel and convenience therefore which its growing importance required. I would therefore recommend that legislation be had establishing it as a national park.[141]

The Secretary realized the inadequacy of his powers over the Canyon. A need was being felt for some organized control for the happiness and comfort of the tourists.

Among other things, there was need of automobile roads along the rim. The first automobile was driven to the Canyon in 1902 by Oliver Lippincott.[142] The success of the trip encouraged J. G. Verkamp to take a trip East to investigate the practicability of the automobile, then in its infancy. He thought that if possible, he might establish a motor-bus line to the Canyon from Flagstaff. But it was still too early in the life of the automobile to hope for the successful operation of such a line.[143] However, by 1910 the automobile was becoming a popular public carrier. Flagstaff's automobile club began a movement for a permanent automobile road to the Canyon, via Grand View Point. The wagon roads along the rim were being improved by the Santa Fe, but there was still need for a great deal of work and the government refused to appropriate funds for it.

---

[140]President Taft visited the Grand Canyon on October 13, 1909.

[141]*Coconino Sun*, November 26, 1909.

[142]Austin, E., *op. cit.*, p. 42.

[143]*Coconino Sun*, February 1, 1902.

Creation of Grand Canyon National Park

In 1910 Senator Flint introduced a bill in Congress to set aside the Grand Canyon as a national park. He had the support of President Taft in this move.[144] However, his bill met with the same fate as its predecessors.

After Arizona's admission to the Union as a state in 1912, some of Flagstaff's business men began to urge their Congressmen and Senators to work for a Grand Canyon National Park. There men, however, were still in the minority and were severely criticized as seeking solely their own benefit by an enlarged tourist trade.[145]

By 1915 Phoenix, Arizona joined in the Park movement. Its Chamber of Commerce on June 24, 1915, passed a resolution saying; "We earnestly recommend the creation and establishment of the Grand Canyon of Arizona National Park."[146]

This was the year of the San Francisco World's Fair. Arizona was receiving an unprecedented influx of tourists from the entire country. The Grand Canyon was one of Arizona's chief attractions for these people. Phoenix, as well as the rest of the state, wanted to seize this opportunity of spreading word of Arizona's scenic wonders. To have a national park within her boundaries would serve as a powerful medium of advertising.

Travelers visited the Grand Canyon in such numbers the accommodations proved insufficient to care for all of them. In an effort to overcome this deficiency, the Forest Service encouraged all who cared to, to come to the Canyon and operate livery establishments. This unqualified request brought many rough and undesirable characters to the Canyon.[147] The competition grew so strong that considerable unpleasantness resulted. The situation called for some sort of solution, but no one agency had the authority to impose much needed regulation.

The Santa Fe, which had suffered from the general disorder, began to press for government action. It refused to spend more money until the latter took a more decided interest in the Canyon. It claimed to have invested $1,000,000.00 already on the branch line to the Canyon and in providing hotel facilities, roads and trails.[148]

The people of northern Arizona were growing less belligerent in their attitude toward the National Park idea. They began to realize it was practically a necessity. But they would not give up their active opposition in 1916, because they felt that the proposed boundaries for the park included too much land. They feared that the government would set aside a vast area to make a good showing and deprive them of good grazing lands.[149]

Congressman Hayden from Arizona appreciated the attitude of the people of northern Arizona. He was in sympathy with their efforts to prevent the National Government from grabbing a large portion of their grazing lands. The proposed

---

[144]*Coconino Sun*, February 4, 1910.

[145]Ibid., September 13, 1912.

[146]Ibid., July 23, 1915.

[147]Kolb, E., *Personal Interview*, March 18, 1940.

[148]*Coconino Sun*, November 17, 1916.

[149]Ibid. November 17, 1916.

boundaries included much land which would be of little or no value to the park, but was desirable to stockmen. With this in mind he drafted a bill creating the Grand Canyon National Park. By his bill the boundaries of the park were drawn in toward the rim, greatly reducing the area included in the earlier boundary proposals.

On February 26, 1919, the act creating Grand Canyon National Park was passed. This was essentially the same bill drafted by Hayden two years before. The act reads in part as follows:

> Be it enacted by the Senate and House of Representatives of the United States in Congress assembled, That there is hereby reserved and withdrawn from settlement, occupancy, or disposal under the laws of The United States and dedicated and set apart as a public park for the benefit and enjoyment of the people, under the name of the "Grand Canyon National Park."
>
> That all concessions for hotels, camps, transportation, and other privileges of every kind and nature for the accommodation or entertainment of visitors shall be left at public bidding to the best and the most responsible bidder.
>
> That nothing herein contained shall affect any valid existing claim, location entry under the land laws of the United States, whether for homestead, mineral, right of way, or any other purpose whatsoever, or shall affect the rights of any such claimant, locator or entryman to the full use and enjoyment of his land and nothing herein contained shall affect, diminish, or impair the right and authority of the County of Coconino... to levy and collect tolls for the passage of livestock over and upon the Bright Angel Toll Road or Trail, and the Secretary of the Interior is hereby authorized to negotiate with the said county... for purchase of said Bright Angel Trail and all rights therein...
>
> ...the Secretary of the Interior is authorized... to permit the prospecting, development and utilization of the mineral resources of said park...[150]

By this act Grand Canyon became the seventeenth of the twenty-five national parks in the United States.[151] Its area is 1,009 square miles or approximately 645,000 acres. It stretches for fifty-six miles to the west, starting at the juncture of the Grand and Marble Canyons. Through it winds the Colorado River for one hundred and five miles.[152]

---

[150]Tolson, H., *op. cit.*, pp. 205-209.

[151]Gustafson, A .F., *Conservation in the United States*, p. 235.

[152]Tillotson. M. R., *Grand Canyon Country*, p. 49.

42

National Park Service Control of the Grand Canyon National Park

Grand Canyon National Park was placed under the National Park Service, which had been established on August 25, 1916. Previous to that date, national parks had had no coordinated administration. In the April following the creation of the Park Service, funds were appropriated for its establishment, and Stephen T. Mather was appointed Director.[153]

The philosophy of the National Park Service may be gleaned from a letter written in May, 1918 by Secretary of the Interior, Lane to Director Mather,

> The administration policy to which the new service will adhere is based on three broad principles. First, that the national parks must be maintained in absolutely unimpaired form for the use of future generations as well as those of our own times; second, that they are set apart for the use, observation, health and pleasure of the people; and third, that national interest must dictate all decisions affecting public or private enterprise in the parks... The educational as well as the recreational use of the national parks should be encouraged in every practicable way.[154]

With the creation of the national park at Grand Canyon the National Park Service set to work immediately to improve the area and eliminate, as far as possible all outsiders, who were the source of disorder. Those with legitimate claims, of course, were protected by the act creating the park. Most of these fought the Government's control to the end.

Because it was unable to buy the Bright Angel Trail from the county, the Park Service began construction of a new trail. This was known as The Yaki or Kaibab Trail. It was three miles east of the Bright Angel Trail and led to the river opposite the mouth of the Bright Angel Creek. Three quarters of a mile up the Bright Angel Creek, Phantom Ranch was constructed by the Fred Harvey Company. This is a guest ranch. These two projects were completed in 1921.[155]

In the winter of 1927-28 a rigid suspension bridge was built across the Colorado River, replacing the swinging bridge which had first been built. This same winter the Kaibab Trail was completed up Bright Angel Canyon to the north rim.[156] This part of the trail was built to accommodate the visitors approaching the Canyon from the north. Accommodations for the visitors on the north rim were also erected in the winter of 1927-28 by the Utah Parks Company, a subsidiary of the Union Pacific Railroad Company. The new hotel named Grand Canyon Lodge, was built on Bright Angel Point on the north rim directly opposite El Tovar Hotel on the south rim.

---

[153]Wilbur, R. L., and Du Puy, W. A., *Conservation in the Department of the Interior*, pp. 96-106.

[154]Ibid., pp. 107-108.

[155]Kolb, E., *Personal Interview*, March 18, 1940.

[156]*Circular of General Information Regarding Grand Canyon National Park*, p. 9.

The Union Pacific Company signed a twenty year contract with The National Park Service on October 13, 1927, for a concession to operate hotel, autobus and saddle-horse services on the north rim. On August 20th of the same year they received a fifty year franchise from the county of Coconino for telephone and telegraph services.[157]

This is the only organization to operate on the north rim. A few previous attempts were made, but none succeeded. This hotel operates only during the summer months, as the rim is closed to travel the rest of the year due to heavy snows.

With tourist accommodations well arranged on both rims and the Park Service functioning smoothly, the Grand Canyon was making fine progress. But there were still the miners to cause irritation. Finally on January 26, 1931, Congress passed the following law to put an end to this trouble. "Hereafter no permit, license, lease, or other authorization for the prospecting, development, or utilization of the mineral resources within the... Grand Canyon National Park, Arizona, shall be granted or made."[158]

Later Developments Under Federal Direction of the Grand Canyon National Park

This act and the one creating the park completely eliminated any future private enterprise in the park, except by permission of the Park Service or on land which had been patented. However, the Federal Government was not yet satisfied with the extent of the area under its control. On December 22, 1932, the Grand Canyon National Monument was created. It included an area of 273,145 acres west of the boundaries of the Grand Canyon National Park.[159] Again in 1935 a bill was introduced into Congress which would abolish Grand Canyon National Monument and add approximately fifty-seven per cent of its area to the Grand Canyon National Park.[160] This bill was not passed. Some Grand Canyon territory was returned to the public domain on April 4, 1940. By Presidential proclamation a considerable portion of the Grand Canyon National Monument, lying northwest of the park, was relinquished by the Federal Government.[161] The action on the part of the National Government which has aroused protest from the people of northern Arizona at present (1940) is its attempt to take possession of William Randolph Hearst's property on the Canyon's rim. It is feared that this is but one step toward the seizure of all private property within the park boundaries. There are only four such pieces of property besides that owned by the railroad,[162] but the county does not want to lose the tax revenue derived from them. As yet no action has been taken in the matter. The case is still in court.

---

[157]*Minutes of the Board of Supervisors, Coconino County*, Vol. V, pp. 366-367.

[158]Tolson, *op. cit.*, p. 214.

[159]*Annual Report of the Secretary of the Interior*, 1933, p. 160.

[160]*Annual Report of the Secretary of the Interior*, 1936, p. 110.

[161]*Coconino Sun*, April 19, 1940.

[162]These are owned by Martin Buggeln estate, William Randolph Hearst, Daniel Hogan and Ed Hamilton estate.

Grand Canyon National Park is now one of the best known of the nation's parks. Between 300,000 and 400,000 people visit it yearly. Every effort is made to preserve it in all its natural beauty. Although most of the visitors stay for only a day, more and more people are prolonging their visits for a week or longer. The fine trails and roads make accessible spots deserving of a visit. Geologists, botanists, archaeologists, etc., find abundant opportunity to make first hand studies of nature in an undisturbed state. Nature lovers with no technical knowledge will find countless opportunities for pleasure in this great natural and scenic vacation land.

BIBLIOGRAPHY

Books

1. Adams, Ward R., *History of Arizona*, Vol. II, Record Publishing Company, Phoenix, 1930.
2. Bancroft, Hubert Howe, *History of Arizona and New Mexico*, The History Company, San Francisco, 1889.
   _____, *History of California*, Vol. III, A. L. Bancroft and Company, San Francisco, 1885.
   _____, *History of Utah*, The History Company, San Francisco, 1889.
3. Bartlett, John Russell, *Personal narrative of explorations and incidents in Texas, New Mexico, California, Sonora and Chihuahua*, Vol. II, D. Appleton and Company, New York, 1854.
4. Barnes, Will C., *Arizona Place Names*, University of Arizona, Tucson, Arizona, 1935.
5. Beckwourth, James P., *The Life and Adventures of James P. Beckwourth*, Alfred A. Knopf, New York, 1931.
6. Bishop, Morris Gilbert, *The Odyssey of Cabeza de Vaca*, The Century Company, New York and London, 1933.
7. Blackmar, Frank Wilson, *Spanish Institutions of the Southwest*, The John Hopkins Press, Baltimore, 1891.
8. Bolton, Herbert Eugene, *Ansa's California Expedition*, Vol. I, University of California Press, Berkeley 1930.
   _____, *Guide to Materials for the History of the United States in the Principal Archives of Mexico*, Carnegie Institution of Washington, Washington, D.C., 1913.
   _____, *Outpost of Empire*, A. A. Knopf, New York, 1931.
   _____, *Rim of Christendom*, The Macmillan Company, New York, 1936.
   _____, *Spanish Borderlands*, Yale University Press, New Haven, 1921.
   _____, *Spanish Explorations of the Southwest*, C. Scribner's Sons, New York, 1916.
   _____, and Marshall, Thomas Maitland, *The Colonization of North America*, The Macmillan Company, New York, 1920.
9. Bonsal, Stephen, *Edward Fitzgerald Beale, A Pioneer in the Path of Empire 1822-1903*, G.P. Putnam's Sons, New York, 1912.
10. Bradley, Glenn D., *Winning the Southwest, A Story of Conquest*, A.C. McClure and Company, Chicago, 1912.
11. Brewerten, George Douglas, *Overland with Kit Carson, A Narrative of the Old Spanish Trail in '48*, Coward-McClunn, Inc., New York, 1930.
12. Chapman, Charles Edward, *Catalogue of Materials in the Archive General de Indias*, University of California Press, Berkeley, 1919.
   _____, *History of California*, The Macmillan Company, New York, 1921.
13. Chittenden, Hiram Martin, *The American Fur Trade of the Far West*, Vol. I and II, Rufus Rockwell Wilson, Inc. 1936.

14. Connors, Jo, *Who's Who in Arizona*, Arizona Daily Star, Tucson, Arizona, 1913.

15. Coues, Elliott, *On the Trail of a Spanish Pioneer*, Vol. II, F.P. Harper, New York, 1900.

16. Dale, Harrison Clifford, *The Ashley-Smith Exploration and the Discovery of a Route to the Pacific 1822-1829*, The Arthur H. Clark Company, Cleveland, 1918.

17. Dawson, Thomas Fulton, *The Grand Canyon*, Government Printing Office, Washington, D.C., 1917.

18. Dellenbaugh, Frederick Samuel, *A Canyon Voyage*, G. P. Putnam's Sons, New York, 1908.

_____, *The Romance of the Colorado River*, G. P. Putnam's Sons, New York, 1909.

19. De Long, Sidney Randolph, *History of Arizona*, The Whitaker and Ray Company, San Francisco, 1905.

20. Engelhardt, Zephyria, *The Franciscans in Arizona*, Holy Childhood Indian School, Harbor Springs, Michigan, 1889.

21. Farish, Thomas Edwin, *History of Arizona*, Vol. I and II, The Filmer Brothers Electrotype Company, San Francisco, 1918.

22. Favour, Alpheus H., *Old Bill Williams: Mountain Man*, The University of North Carolina Press, Raleigh, 1936.

23. Flint, Timothy, ed., *The Personal Narrative of James O. Pattie of Kentucky*, R.R. Connelley and Sons Company, Chicago, 1930.

24. Freeman, Lewis Ransome, *The Colorado River Yesterday, Today and Tomorrow*, Dodd, Mead and Company, New York, 1923.

_____, *Down the Grand Canyon*, Williams Heinemann Ltd., London, 1924.

25. Goodwin, Cardinal, *The Trans-Mississippi West*, D. Appleton, New York, 1924.

26. Gustofson, A. F., Ries, H., Guise, D. H., and Hamilton, W. J., *Conservation in the United States*, Comstock Publishing Company, Inc., Cornell Heights, Ithaca, New York, 1939.

27. Hafen, Le Roy R., and Ghont, W. J., *Broken Hand*, The Old West Publishing Company, Denver, 1905.

28. Hamilton, William T., *My Sixty Years on the Plains*, Forest and Stream Publishing Company, New York, 1905.

29. Higgins, C. A., Powell, John Wesley, and Lummis, Charles Fletcher, *Titan of Chasms The Grand Canyon of Arizona*, Passenger Department of the Santa Fe, Chicago, 1910.

30. Hinton, Richard Josiah, *Handbook of Arizona*, American News Company, New York, 1878.

31. James, George Wharton, *The Grand Canyon of Arizona: How to See It*, Little, Brown and Company, Boston, 1910.

_____, *In and Around the Grand Canyon*, Little, Brown and Company, Boston, 1903.

32. Jenson, Andrew, *Church Chronology A Record of Important Events*, Second Edition, Deseret News, Salt Lake City, Utah, 1899.

33. Lummis, Charles Fletcher, *The Spanish Pioneers*, A. C. McClurg and Company, Chicago, 1893.

34. McClintock, James H., *Arizona, Pre-Historic-Aboriginal-Pioneer-Modern*, Vol. I, II and III, The S.J. Clarke Publishing Company, Chicago, 1916.
_____, *Mormon Settlement in Arizona*, The Manufacturing Stationers Inc., Phoenix, Arizona, 1921.

35. Nicholson, George T., *The Grand Canyon of Arizona*, Poole Brothers, Chicago, 1906.

36. Paxson, Frederick Logan, *History of the American Frontier 1763-1893*. The Riverside Press, Cambridge, 1924.

37. Peter, De Witt Clinton, *Pioneer Life and Frontier Adventures*, Estes and Lauriat, Boston, 1883.

38. Powell, John Wesley, *Canyons of the Colorado*, Flood and Vincent, Meadeville, Pennsylvania, 1895.

39. Riegel, Robert E., *America Moves West*, Henry Holt and Company, New York, 1930.

40. Richardson, Rupert Norval, and Rister, Carl Coke, *The Greater Southwest*, The Arthur H. Clark Company, Glendale, California, 1934.

41. Robidoux, Orral Messmore, *Memorial to the Robidoux Brothers*, Smith-Greaves Company, Kansas City, 1924.

42. Ruxton, George Frederick, *In the Old West*, The Macmillan Company, New York, 1922.

43. Sauer, Carl, "The Road to Cibola"; *Ibero-Americana: 3*, University of California Press, Berkeley, 1932.

44. Simpson, James H., *Coronado's March*, Government Printing Office, Washington, D.C. 1884.

45. Stanton, Robert Brewster, *Colorado River Controversies*, Dodd, Mead and Company, New York, 1932.

46. Thwaites, Reuben Gold, *Early Western Travels 1748-1846*, Vol. XVIII, The Arthur H. Clark Company, Cleveland, Ohio.

47. Tillotson, Miner Raymond, and Taylor, Frank J., *Grand Canyon Country*, Stanford University Press, 1930.

48. Tolson, Hillory A., *Laws relating to the National Park Service, the National Parks and Monuments*, Government Printing Office, Washington, D.C., 1935.

49. Vandiveer, Clarence A., *The Fur Trade and Early Western Exploration*, The Arthur H. Clark Company, Cleveland, 1929.

50. Van Dyke, John C., *The Grand Canyon of the Colorado*, Charles Scribner's Sons, New York, 1924.

51. Vestal, Stanley, *Kit Carson*, Houghton Mifflin Company, Boston, 1928.

52. Wilbur, Ray Lyman, and Du Puy, William Atherton, *Conservation in the Department of the Interior*, Government Printing Office, Washington, D.C. 1932.

53. Woods, G. K., *Personal Impression of the Grand Cañon of the Colorado River Near Flagstaff, Arizona*, The Whitaker and Ray Company, San Francisco, 1899.

54. Wyllys, Rufus Kay, *Pioneer Padre*, Southwest Press, Dallas, 1935.

Magazine Articles

1. Anonymous, "The Story of James White"; *The Outing Magazine*, Vol. L, April, 1907.

   _____, "Through Grand Canyon on a Raft"; *The Outing Magazine*, Vol. LXXII, May 1918.

2. Baldwin, Percy M., "Fray Marcos de Niza and His Discovery of the Seven Cities of Cibola"; *New Mexico Historical Review*, Vol. I, April, 1926.

3. Bandelier, Adolph Francis, "The Discovery of New Mexico by Fray Marcos of Nizza"; *New Mexico Historical Review*, Vol. IV, January, 1929.

4. Bolton, Herbert Eugene, "Escalante in Dixie and the Arizona Strip"; *New Mexico Historical Review*, Vol. III, January, 1928.

5. Brayer, Herbert O., "Peter Heylyn's Cosmography of New Mexico"; *New Mexico Historical Review*, Vol. XI, April, 1936.

6. Cheetham, Francis T., "Kit Carson, Pathbreaker, Patriot and Humanitarian"; *New Mexico Historical Review*, Vol. I, October, 1926.

7. Espinoza, Gilberto, "The Coronado Fourth Centennial"; *The New Mexico Quarterly*, Vol. V., August, 1935.

8. Hammond, George P., "Oñate A Marauder?"; *New Mexico Historical Review*, Vol. X, October, 1935.

9. Hill, Joseph J., "New Light on Pattie and the Southwestern Fur Trade"; *Southwestern Historical Quarterly*, Vol. XXVI, April, 1923.

10. Nims, F.A., "Through Mysterious Cañons of the Colorado"; *The Overland Monthly*, Vol. XIX, March, 1892.

11. Reynolds, Ethan Allen, "In the Whirlpools of the Grand Cañon of the Colorado"; *Cosmopolitan*, Vol. VIII, November, 1889.

12. Warner, Arthur, "Canyons and Camerons"; *Nation*, Vol. 121, October 28, 1925.

Pamphlets

1. Bass, William Wallace, *Adventures in the Canyons of the Colorado*, Grand Canyon, 1920.

2. Cameron, Ralph Henry, *Speeches of the Hon. Ralph H. Cameron of Arizona in the Senate of the United States*, "The Bright Angel Trail"; Government Printing Office, Washington, D.C., 1924.

3. *Circular of General Information Regarding Grand Canyon National Park, Arizona*, Government Printing Office, Washington, D.C., 1929.

4. Noble, Levi F., *The Shinumo quadrangle Grand Canyon district, Arizona*, Government Printing Office, Washington, D.C., 1914.

Newspaper Clippings

1. *Arizona Champion*, Flagstaff, Arizona, January 17, 1885, Vol. II, No. 19, to October 26, 1889, Vol. VII, No. 3.
2. *Arizona Journal-Miner*, Prescott, Arizona, July 30, 1889, Vol. XXXII, No. 119.
3. *Arizona Republic*, Phoenix, Arizona, April Issues for 1908.
4. *Arizona Silver Belt*, Globe, Arizona, January 15 to March 12, 1887, Vol. IX.
5. Austin, Edwin, *Grand Canyon Items from the Arizona Champion and Coconino Sun*, 1886-1914, MS.
6. *Coconino Sun*, Flagstaff, Arizona, June 13, 1891, Vol. VIII, No. 39 to April 19, 1940, Vol. LVIII, No. 24.
7. *Mojave County Miner*, Kingman, Arizona, March 18, 1893, Vol. XI, No 20.
8. *Phoenix Daily Herald*, Phoenix, Arizona, March 8, 1893, Vol. XX, No. 58.
9. *Prescott Courier*, Prescott, Arizona, February Issues for 1919.

Personal Interviews and Letters

1. Babbitt, Charles, J., Flagstaff, Arizona, March 1, 1940.
2. Gilliland, Richard P., Grand Canyon, Arizona, March 21, 1940.
3. Kolb, Emery, Grand Canyon, Arizona, March 18, 1940.
4. Lauzon, Hubert, Grand Canyon, Arizona, March 22 and 26, 1940.
5. Page, John H., Grand Canyon, Arizona, April 13, 1940.
6. Verkamp, John George, Grand Canyon, Arizona, April 11, 1940.
7. Cameron, B. A., to Verkamp, Peggy, Flagstaff, Arizona, April 2, 1940.
8. Gregg, Marie, to Verkamp, Peggy, Flagstaff, Arizona, March 30, 1940.
9. Page, John H., to Verkamp, Peggy, Phoenix, Arizona, April 16, 1940.
10. Standage, C. L., to Fleming, George, Phoenix, Arizona, March 14, 1940.

Official Reports and Documents

1. *Abstract of Title*, No. 1101, Coconino County Abstract Company, Flagstaff, Arizona.
2. Adams, Samuel, "Communications and Report"; *The Miscellaneous Documents of the House of Representatives, 1870-71*, Vol. I, 41st Congress, 3rd Session, Government Printing Office, Washington, D.C., 1871.
3. *Annual Report of the Board of Regents of the Smithsonian Institution for 1875*, Government Printing Office, Washington, D.C., 1876.
4. *Annual Report of the Secretary of the Interior for the Fiscal Years ended June 30, 1933 and June 30, 1936*, Government Printing Office, Washington, D.C., 1933 and 1936.
5. California Colorado River Commission, *Colorado River and the Boulder Canyon Project*, California State Printing Office, Sacramento, 1931.
6. *Files of Civil Cases, District Court of the Fourth Judicial District of the Territory of Arizona, in and for the County of Coconino*, Cases Nos. 641, 725, 729, 750, 963, 1048, MSS, County Court House, Flagstaff, Arizona.

7. Ives, Joseph C., *Report upon the Colorado River of the West*, Government Printing Office, Washington, D.C., 1861.
8. Kinsey, Don Jackson, *The River of Destiny*, Department of Water and Power, Los Angeles, 1928.
9. *Minutes of the Board of Supervisors of the County of Coconino, Territory of Arizona*, Vols. I, II, III, IV, V, MSS, County Court House, Flagstaff, Arizona.
10. Powell, John Wesley, *Report of Explorations in 1873 of the Colorado of the West and Its Tributaries*, Government Printing Office, Washington, D.C., 1874.
11. *Proceedings of the National Parks Conference*, Government Printing Office, Washington, D.C., 1917.
12. *Record of Articles of Incorporation, Coconino County, Territory of Arizona*, Vol. I, County Recorder's Office, Flagstaff, Arizona.
13. *Record of Deeds*, Books 32, 55, 56, County Recorder's Office, Flagstaff, Arizona.
14. *Reports of Cases, Argued and Determined in the Supreme Court of the Territory of Arizona*, Vol. XII.
15. *Session Laws of the Fifteenth Legislative Assembly of the Territory of Arizona*, 1889.
16. *Session Laws of the Twentieth Legislative Assembly of the Territory of Arizona*, 1899.
17. *Session Laws of the Twenty-Fourth Legislative Assembly of the Territory of Arizona*, 1907.
18. *Session Laws of the Legislature of the State of Arizona, Acts and Resolutions of the Fourth Special Session Eighth Legislature of the State of Arizona*, 1927.
19. Sitgreaves, Lorenzo, *Report of an Expedition Down the Zuni and Colorado Rivers*, Senate Printers, Washington, D.C., 1854.
20. *Statutes at Large of the United States of America*, Vols. XVIII, XXVII, XXXV.
21. Wheeler, George M., *Report Upon United States Geographical Surveys West of the One Hundredth Meridian*, Vol. I, Government Printing Office, Washington, D.C., 1889.
22. Winship, George Parker, "The Coronado Expedition, 1540-1542"; *Fourteenth Annual Report of the Bureau of Ethnology 1892-93*, Government Printing Office, Washington, D.C., 1893.

INDEX

Alarcon, Hernando, 1, 3
Albuquerque, New Mexico, 3, 24
Anita mines, 19
Anita, Arizona, 23, 25
Anza, Captain Juan Bautista de, 4
Arizona, 1, 8, 9, 10, 11, 14, 18, 25,
   27, 34, 35, 38, 39, 42, 45
Arizona Legislature, 12, 25, 32, 34
Arizona, admission as state, 42
asbestos, 12, 14, 19, 25
Ash Fork, Arizona, 23, 26
Ashley, William Henry, 5
Ashurst, Henry F., 14, 32
Ashurst, William Henry, 14, 16
Atlantic and Pacific Railroad, 10, 12,
   15, 22, 23
Aubineau, Julius, 20
automobile road, 27, 40
automobile, first, 40
Ayer, Edward E., 10

Babbitt Brothers Trading Company, 26
Babbitt, David, 20
Barbour , Henry P., 20
Barman, A., 20
Barstow, California, 24
Bass Camp, 16, 25, 27
Bass Trail, 16
Bass, William Wallace, 15, 23, 25, 26
Beaver Dam Mountains, 6
Berby, Lieutenant George H., 7
Berry, Peter D., 16, 19, 20, 25, 29
Bill Williams Fork, 7
Black Canyon of the Colorado, 5, 7
Boucher Trail, 33
Boucher, Louis, 33
Breen, S. R., 29
Bright Angel Camp, 24, 26
Bright Angel Canyon, 44
Bright Angel Creek, 20, 29, 44
Bright Angel Hotel, 25, 26, 29, 31
Bright Angel Point, 44
Bright Angel Toll Road, 30, 31, 33, 34,
   43

Bright Angel Trail, 16, 19, 22, 23, 29,
   30, 31, 32, 33, 34, 35, 36, 39, 43,
   44
Brown, Frank Mason, 8
Buena Guia, 3
Buggeln, Martin, 26, 29, 30, 31, 39
Bureau of Topographical Engineers, 7

Cabeza de Vaca, 1
California, 4, 5, 6, 9, 22
Cameron Bill, 32
Cameron, Niles J., 16, 19
Cameron, Ralph H., 14, 20, 25, 29, 30,
   31, 32, 33, 34, 35, 36
Cameron, Ralph H., born, 35
Camp Verde, Arizona, 11
Canyon Copper Company, 20, 25
Cardenas, Garcia, 2, 3
Carson, Christopher "Kit", 6
Casteñada, Pedro, 2
Cataract Canyon, 4, 9, 10
Cedar Station, 22
Chicago Academy of Science., 7
Cibola, 1, 2, 3
Civil War, 11
Cobb, S., 27
Coconino County, 19, 24, 29, 31, 32,
   33, 34, 37, 38, 43, 45
Coconino County, Board of
Supervisors, 30, 31, 33, 34, 38
Coconino Cycling Club, 23
Colorado, 4, 8
Colorado Grand Canyon Mining and
Improvement Company, 17
Colorado River, 3, 4, 5, 6, 7, 8, 9, 10,
   14, 19, 20, 27, 29, 38, 43, 44
Conchos River, 3
Confederate Army, 11
copper, 12, 14, 19, 25
Coronado, Francisco, 1, 2, 3
Cram, John, 27
Crossing of the Fathers, 5, 10
Crozier, S., 14
Culiacan, 1
curio business, 26, 29

Denver, Colorado, 17
Department of Interior, 40
Diamond Creek, 8, 15
Doe, E. M., 24
Dorantes, Andres, 1

Eckles, James H., 19
El Tovar Hotel, 24, 26, 33, 44
Escalante, Father, 4, 5
Espejo, Antonio, 3
Estevan, 1
expedition, Coronado, 1, 24
expedition, Florida, 1
expedition, Oñate, 3
expedition, Spanish, 1
expedition, Stanton, 17
Explorer, steamship, 7
expulsion of the Jesuits, 3

Father Kino, 3, 4
Ferguson, R. A., 19
Ferguson, Robert, 16, 29
Ferrall, L. L., 31, 32
Flagstaff and Grand Canyon Railroad,
    12
Flagstaff Board of Trade, 22
Flagstaff's automobile club, 40
Flagstaff, Arizona, 10, 11, 12, 13, 14,
    16, 17, 18, 20, 22, 23, 25, 26, 33,
    37, 40
Flint, Senator, 42
Fort Mojave, 8
Fort Yuma, 7
Foster, R. W., 20
Franciscan Friar, 1, 3
Fray Marcos, 1
Fray Rodriquez, 3
Fred Harvey Company, 24, 26, 31, 44
Fredonia, Arizona, 27
Frier, Thomas, 16

Gabel, T. R., 22
Gale, E. I., 19
Galeras, Juan, 2
Garces, Francisco, 4, 5

Gila River, 5, 6
gold, 14
Grand Canyon Electric Power
Company, 20
Grand Canyon Forest Reserve, 18, 32
Grand Canyon Game Reserve, 40
Grand Canyon Hotel, 23, 39
Grand Canyon Lodge, 44
Grand Canyon National Forest, 39
Grand Canyon National Monument, 39,
    40, 45
Grand Canyon National Park, 33, 34,
    36, 37, 38, 42, 43, 44, 45, 46
Grand Canyon of the Colorado, 3, 11,
    12, 22, 29, 40
Grand Canyon Railway, 24
Grand Canyon Railway Company, 29
Grand Canyon Reserve, 37
Grand Canyon stage line, 26
Grand Canyon Village, 11, 16, 23, 26
Grand Canyon, Arizona, 16
Grand River, 5, 6, 8
Grand View Hotel, 25
Grand View Point, 19, 40
Grand View Trail, 16, 25
Grand Wash, 9
Great Salt Lake, 4
Green River, 5, 6, 8
Green River City, Wyoming, 8
guest ranch, 44
Gulf of California, 1, 3, 8, 27
Gulf of Mexico, 1
Gunnison Valley, 6
Guzman, Nuño, 1

Hamblin, Jacob, 9, 10
Hance Asbestos Mining Company, 19
Hance Hotel, 23, 25
Hance Trail, 14, 16
Hance, John, 11, 12, 14, 19, 23, 31
Harrison, Benjamin, 18, 37, 40
Havasupai Canyon, 4
Havasupai Indians, 10
Hayden Bill, 33
Hayden, Carl, 42, 43

Hearst, William Randolph, 20
Hermit Basin, 33
Hills, George E., 19
Hitchcock, E. A., 32
Hopi House, 26
Hopi Indians, 10
Hopi villages, 9, 10
House Trail, 29
Hull's tank, 30
Hull, Phillip, 10
Hull, William, 10, 11

Indian Gardens, 26, 29, 36
Ives, Lieutenant Joseph Christmas, 7, 9

Jackson, David E., 5

Kaibab Plateau, 26
Kaibab Trail, 44
Kanab Canyon, 8
Kanab, Utah, 8, 27
Kansas, 3
Kansas City, Missouri, 24
Kenna, Edward D., 19
Kibbey, Governor, 32
Kingman, Arizona, 4
Kolb brothers, 26, 27
Kolb, Ellsworth, 26
Kolb, Emery, 26

land route to California, 4
Last Chance Mine, 19, 20, 25
Lee's Ferry, 8
Lewis and Clark Expedition, 5
Lippincott, Oliver, 40
Little Colorado River, 7, 19
Little Springs, 22
Lombard, Goode and Company, 18, 19,
   24
Louisiana Purchase, 5
lower California, 3
Lund, Utah, 27

Maine, Arizona, 34
Maldonado, Alonso, 1

Marble Canyon, 43
Marshall, John, 16
Massachusetts, 19
Mather, Stephen T., 44
McClure, C. H., 16
McMillan, Thomas, 19
Melgosa, Captain, 2
Mendoza, Antonio, 1
Mexico, 3
mining claim, Cape Horn, 35, 39
mining claim, Golden Eagle, 35, 39
missionary, Franciscan, 4
missionary, Jesuit, 3
missionary, Mormon, 9, 10
Missouri, 11
Missouri River, 5
Mojave Indians, 4, 10
Mojave River, 5, 6, 7
Mojave Valley, 9
Monterey, California, 4
Moqui Station, 22
Moqui Trail, 9, 10
Morris, J. S., 12
Mountain Meadows, Utah, 6, 9
Mystic Spring Trail, 26

Narvarez, Panfilo, 1
National Old Trails Highway, 34
national park, 9, 22, 34, 37, 40, 42, 43,
   44
National Park Service, 44, 45
Nevada, 6
New Spain, 3
Niza, Marcos de, 1
North Rim, 25, 26, 27, 38, 40, 44, 45
Nuebo Canfran, 4

O'Neill, William Owen "Buckey", 18
Old Spanish Trail, 6

Page, John H., 25, 39
Paria River, 8
park boundaries, 34, 42, 43, 45
Pattie, James Ohio, 5
Peach Springs, Arizona, 15, 22, 23

Peters, W. H., 33
Phantom Ranch, 44
Phoenix, Arizona, 42
Pierce's Ferry, 10
Pimeria Alta, 3
Pittsburgh, Pennsylvania, 26
Point Sublime, 27
Powell, Major John Wesley, 7, 8
Prescott, Arizona, 18
Puerto de Bucareli, 4

Red Canyon Trail, 14
Ridenour, William, 14
Rio de Palmas, 1
Rio de San Antonia, 4
Rio Grande, 3
Rio Jabesua, 4
Rocky Mountain Fur Company, 5
Rodriquez, Augustin, 3
Roosevelt, Theodore, 39, 40
Rowe, Sanford, 23
Runke, Walter, 34

Salt Lake City, Utah, 9, 10
Salt Lake Railroad, 27
San Diego, California, 5
San Francisco Mountains, 9
San Francisco Peaks, 22
San Juan River, 6
Santa Barbara, mission, 3
Santa Fe and Grand Canyon Railroad, 18, 23, 24
Santa Fe Land and Improvement Company, 26
Santa Fe Railroad, 19, 23, 24, 26, 33, 35, 39, 41, 42
Santa Fe, New Mexico, 3, 4, 6
Secretary of the Interior, 29, 33, 43
Secretary of the Interior, Ballinger, 40
Secretary of the Interior, Hitchcock, 32
Secretary of the Interior, Lane, 44
Sevier Valley, 5
Shinumo Canyon, 26
Sierra Nevada, 4
Sinaloa Valley, 1

Sitgreaves, Captain Lorenzo, 7
Smith, Byron L., 19
Smith, Jedediah S., 5
Smith, Marcus A., 18
Sonora Valley, 1
South Rim, 3, 9, 15, 27, 44
Spanish Conquistadors, 24
Stanton, Robert Brewster, 8, 17
Stone, Attorney General, 36
Sublette, William, 5
Summit Hotel, 25
Supreme Court of Arizona, 25, 30
Supreme Court of the United States, 36
suspension bridge, 44

Taft, William Howard, 40, 42
Tanner Trail, 14, 16
Tanner, Seth B., 14
Taos, New Mexico, 6
telegraph services, 45
telephone service, 45
Tennessee, 11
Territory of Arizona, 39
Texas, 1
Thurber, J. W., 19, 23
Tolfree, J. H., 19, 23
toll road, 17, 29, 30, 32, 33, 34
tolls, collection, 29, 30, 31, 32, 33, 43
tourist accommodations, 11, 12, 22, 23, 25, 33, 40, 45
tourist attractions, 9, 14, 15, 22, 37
tourist guide, 11, 15
tourist resort, 11, 20
tourist trade, 17, 26, 42
tourist travel, 12, 14, 20, 23, 26, 27, 28
tourist, first, 10
tourists, 9, 11, 14, 15, 25, 26, 27, 37, 42
Tovar, Pedro, 2
Tusayan, 2, 4

Union Pacific Railroad Company., 44
United States Congress, 25
Utah, 5, 9, 10, 27, 38

Utah Lake, 5
Utah Legislature, 38
Utah Parks Company, 44

Vegas Wash, 7
Vera Cruz, Mexico, 1
Verkamp, J. G., 26, 40
Viceroy of Mexico, 1
Virgin River, 5, 6, 8

War Department, 7, 40
Wasatch Range, 6
Wheeler, Captain George M., 8
Whipple, Lieutenant Amiel Weeks, 7
Williams, Arizona, 14, 15, 16, 17, 18,
    23, 26
Wolfskill, William, 6
Wolley, Royal, 27
Woolley, E. D., 27
World's Fair, Chicago, 19
World's Fair, San Francisco, 42
Wyoming, 5, 27

Yaki Trail, 44
Yellowstone National Park, 37
Young, Brigham, 9
Young, Ewing, 5, 6

Zuni Indians, 2
Zuni River, 7